Have you lost 6% to 7% of your savings without realizing it?

Over the past ten years, if you left your money in a 5¼% savings account, you lost 6% to 7% of your savings. And it didn't have to be that way; there are ways to protect yourself, ways to make money rather than lose money. Don't let the same thing happen over the *next* ten years.

Economically, we are living in a new environment in which the old rules, principles and strategies no longer apply. Not only have things changed drastically, but they continue to change every day without warning. This book teaches you the new rules of the changing financial game, and gives you sound recommendations for your future investments.

EVERYBODY'S INVESTMENT BOOK

D1548105

Bantam Books of Related Interest
Ask your bookseller for the books you have missed

ALL YOU NEED TO KNOW ABOUT BANKS by John A. Cook
   and Robert Wool
ALMOST EVERYONE'S GUIDE TO ECONOMICS by John
   Kenneth Galbraith and Nicole Salinger
THE COMING CURRENCY COLLAPSE by Jerome F. Smith
THE COMPLETE BOOK OF HOME BUYING by Michael
   Sumichrast and Ronald G. Shafer
THE DOW-JONES IRWIN GUIDE TO ESTATE PLANNING
   by William C. Clay, Jr.
HIGH FINANCE ON A LOW BUDGET by Mark Skousen
HOW TO GET FREE TAX HELP by Matthew Lesko
MOLLOY'S LIVE FOR SUCCESS by John T. Molloy
MONEYWISE by Mimi Brien
184 BUSINESSES ANYONE CAN START AND MAKE A LOT
   OF MONEY by Chase Revel
THE ROBERT HALF WAY TO GET HIRED IN TODAY'S
   JOB MARKET
WILLIAM E. DONOGHUE'S COMPLETE MONEY MARKET
   GUIDE

QUANTITY PURCHASES

Companies, professional groups, churches, clubs and other
organizations may qualify for special terms when ordering
24 or more copies of this title. For information, contact the
Direct Response Department, Bantam Books, 666 Fifth
Avenue, New York, N.Y. 10103. Phone (212) 765-6500.

EVERYBODY'S INVESTMENT BOOK*

*How to Invest up to $5,000 Even If You Don't Have It

**Edward Malca
and
Sandra Choron**

BANTAM BOOKS
TORONTO · NEW YORK · LONDON · SYDNEY

Neither the author nor the publisher guarantees or suggests that anything in this book is a definite ticket to success. The book merely furnishes information to potential investors to assist in evaluating various investment opportunities which are broadly available.

EVERYBODY'S INVESTMENT BOOK*
*HOW TO INVEST UP TO $5,000 EVEN IF YOU DON'T HAVE IT
A Bantam Book / May 1984

All rights reserved.
Copyright © 1984 by Edward Malca.
Cover art copyright © 1984 by Bantam Books, Inc.
This book may not be reproduced in whole or in part, by mimeograph or any other means, without permission.
For information address: Bantam Books, Inc.

ISBN 0-553-23952-X

Published simultaneously in the United States and Canada

Bantam Books are published by Bantam Books, Inc. Its trademark, consisting of the words ''Bantam Books'' and the portrayal of a rooster, is Registered in U.S. Patent and Trademark Office and in other countries. Marca Registrada. Bantam Books, Inc., 666 Fifth Avenue, New York, New York 10103.

PRINTED IN THE UNITED STATES OF AMERICA

O   0 9 8 7 6 5 4 3 2 1

For my loving and understanding wife,
Jeanette, and to my delightful son, Andrew.
They have made my life ever so much richer.

E.M.

For my father, who taught me about values.

S.C.

Acknowledgments

The preparation of this book was enhanced by input from a variety of sources. These included conversations with many astute and knowledgeable people, to all of whom I extend my sincere gratitude.

The idea for the book germinated from the personal financial planning seminars I have conducted for the employees of the Con Edison Company of New York, and I am grateful to those connected with that program for their inspiring enthusiasm. In addition, I would like to thank the following individuals:

Professor Peter Gutmann, of the City University of New York, for his genuine interest and encouragement throughout my career; Gilbert A. Millstein, of E. F. Hutton, and David M. Crowther, of Paine Webber, for their helpful advice and materials; and Gail Dobbs for her able typing (she was the first reader of this manuscript to "find" her $5,000).

I am greatly indebted to those friends and relatives who were kind enough to tolerate the day-to-day hardships that this project created. Special thanks go to my wife, Jeanette, and to my son, Andrew, for generously sharing their own time and patience beyond the call of duty.

—EDWARD MALCA

Contents

Preface

In 1982, money market mutual funds were offering an interest rate of up to 16 percent; all-saver certificates yielded a rate of return of over 11 percent and offered investors the additional advantage of up to $1,000 in tax-free income on these profits; and two-year treasury notes were yielding an annual return of 15 percent. Over the past five years, $1,000 placed in a high-risk, special-situation mutual fund earned an average annual return of from 15 percent to 30 percent. And yet, by 1982, Americans had placed over $340 billion of their money in 5¼ percent savings accounts.[1] It is this group of people—those who jeopardized their savings by naïvely investing them in one of the worst possible ways—at whom this book is aimed.

Who are these people? For the most part, it is safe to assume that most of them fall into the following groups: people with moderate incomes who felt that there was little they could do with small sums of money, that "it just didn't matter"; people who grew up believing in a set of economic rules that had simply ceased to make sense in the 1970s; those who were so confused by the many op-

---

[1] *The Wall Street Journal*, September 9, 1982.

tions they heard were available that, unable to choose among them, they didn't choose at all; and those who, facing their later years and anxious about the safety of their investments, believed that banks were the safest investment around.

These people and these fallacies are addressed in *How to Invest up to $5,000 Even If You Don't Have It*. It differs from other investment books in that it is written for those people who have far less money at their disposal than the minimum $10,000 that most other investment books presuppose. Furthermore, it addresses the priorities of its audience more precisely since it offers *specific investment programs* for a variety of groups, all of whom fall within the small-investor category. The results are custom-designed portfolios for people with as much as $5,000—and as little as nothing—at their disposal, along with step-by-step instructions for putting the plans into effect.

It would be impossible and foolhardy to suppose that investment programs can be recommended for anyone without looking further into their lives—at their present situations and priorities and their long-term needs. Although a single thirty-year-old might be in a position to take advantage of a possible 20 percent return on $2,000 placed in a real-estate fund and earn its substantial dividend over the course of six years, a forty-five-year-old married man with a wife and two children to support cannot afford to wait that long for returns on his investment. Nor need he do so. For him, there are other opportunities that not only meet his present need for liquidity but also help to build a foundation for the greater expenses he will have when, say, his children enter college. This is an example of the way in which this book looks at the needs that go hand-in-hand with available investment capital. The general investment guidelines and information contained in this book should be utilized by the investor only in the context of his own particular needs and objectives. Chapter 3 examines such situations more closely. All of the programs recommended in that section address the general needs of all small investors, which include: (1) relative safety of the investments made; (2) flexibility of those investments; (3) the need for liquid funds; (4) return rates that are commensurate with the amount of risk taken; and (5) the need to build a strong foundation for a reliable pension program.

A word about "safety" is appropriate here. It must be remembered that nothing, especially in today's economy, is risk-free. The closest we can come to a completely safe investment would be treasury bills, but as we shall see, even these are not a sure thing. Furthermore, some very low-risk investments are not very good ones—and therefore not recommended here—since their return rate, simply put, is just not worth waiting for. Certainly some of the investments described are what professionals would call "high risk" investments. Although we cannot guarantee the success of these, we can assure readers that the possible risks that accompany such investments will be fully described along with each of the recommendations made and that the risks always will be commensurate with the potential returns. The reader should not take anything in this book as a definite or "sure-fire" ticket to success, but merely as a guide through the furnishing of sufficient information for the unsophisticated investor to evaluate the various investment opportunities which are available to him.

Remember that the advice in this book represents subjective recommendations. In no way is it meant to present *all* the choices available to the small investor. Chapter 12, "Toward Tomorrow," describes ways in which laypeople can keep abreast of new opportunities available to those of modest means (happily, these do come up periodically). But ultimately, after initial investments have been made, readers will have to make their own choices about their lives and their money. It is my hope that this book will eventually help them to make some of those decisions.

1

Introduction: Our Changing Times

There was a time, not too long ago, when a few simple rules provided a good premise for sound money management. Perhaps these are familiar to you:

- Keep your money in a bank; it's safest there.
- Risks are for rich people.
- Don't borrow money unless extenuating circumstances prevail. If you must borrow, pay off your loan as quickly as possible. Mortgages, especially, should be repaid as soon as it becomes financially feasible to do so.
- The best investments are U.S. savings bonds.
- Never spend more than 25 percent of your annual income on housing.
- Social Security will take care of you when you retire.

But today's volatile economy and the resulting runaway inflation rates have changed it all. Consider, for example, the plight of Henry Jones:

Henry Jones grew up believing in the above principles. His father had lived by them, and since Henry, Sr., had managed always to provide for his family in much the

1

same way that his son hoped he could provide for his own some day, young Henry readily accepted the principles when they were handed down to him.

In 1970, at the age of thirty-five, Henry was employed as an engineering assistant earning $10,000 a year. The inflation rate was 5 percent, and Henry, being in the 16 percent tax bracket, paid an annual federal income tax of $500 plus a $525 contribution to Social Security, which he believed would take care of him in his later years. He managed his expenses well, thought little about taxes (except on April 15 of each year), had no trouble making his monthly payments of $207 toward the 7 percent mortgage on his three-bedroom Colonial home, and even managed to set aside a small amount of money each month, which he faithfully deposited in the First National Savings Bank of Anytown. Henry was pleased with the community in which his children were growing up, and Mrs. Jones, not one for expensive luxuries, seemed more than happy with what she had.

Like most of his friends, though, Henry had dreams. He dreamed of being rich one day, and he imagined that if he could work hard enough toward promotions and earn, say, $18,000 by the time he retired, his savings, combined with his Social Security, would earn him a permanent residence on Easy Street.

So Henry deposited his savings in a bank account that earned him an interest rate of 5¼ percent and arranged for monthly payroll deductions toward the purchase of U.S. savings bonds that would someday mature at a 5¼ percent interest rate. Although his 7 percent mortgage extended for thirty years, he tried to reduce it by skimping on entertainment expenses during the course of the year and using the savings, at year's end, to pay off a larger chunk of the money due. How nice it would be one day, he thought, to own the house free and clear.

Henry Jones once received two bank credit cards in the mail. These had been unsolicited, and even though each one of them entitled Henry to a $1,000 credit line, he threw them both in the garbage. "They're not going to suck *me* into debt," he said.

Then there was the time that a friend advised him to refinance his mortgage at 9 percent and use the extra money to become a partner in the mail-order business that his friend was starting. Henry considered it, and it even looked good for a while, but in the end, Henry declined. Such ventures, he thought, were much too risky. Besides, why should he take out a 9 percent mortgage when he already had one at 7 percent? And anyway, that 9 percent mortgage would have brought his annual housing expenditures up to over one third his annual income, and that was definitely too much.

One day, to Henry's delight, part of his dream came true, for it was just ten years later—in 1980—that he was promoted to foreman of his division, and as luck would have it, he surpassed even his own expectations: By now, his salary was doubled, and Henry Jones was earning a nifty $20,000 a year.

But the dream was not as it had seemed. Somehow, Henry felt poorer. He and Mrs. Jones didn't seem able to afford the vacations they had planned, and it was getting harder and harder to make ends meet, let alone maintain that nest egg. Henry's savings bonds were now earning 7 percent a year, yet not since 1976 had he been able to make those annual prepayments on his mortgage, and as if things weren't bad enough, his children were nearing college age, and tuition had certainly gone up since he'd graduated back in 1956. At thirty-five, $20,000 sure had seemed like a lot of money, and yet the luxuries that Henry had thought would accompany all that wealth were still far out of reach. The $6,000 camper he'd pictured himself using on weekend fishing trips now carried a $16,000 price tag, and while his modest Colonial had certainly increased in value a great deal, those four-bedroom ranch homes were untouchable at higher prices and astronomical mortgage rates. Confused and frustrated, Henry Jones shook his head and asked, "Am I crazy? I'm earning more money now than I ever dreamed of making, but it just doesn't add up. Where did I go wrong? Why don't I feel rich?"

Why Henry Doesn't Feel Rich

What happened to Henry is what happened to the rest of us. The following numbers illustrate Henry's situation and perhaps resemble your own:

	1970	1980
Inflation rate	5%	12.4%
Annual income	$10,000	$20,000
Tax bracket	16%	24%
Annual taxes	$500	$2,300
Social Security taxes	$525	$1,300

Quite simply, as the numbers show, Henry's salary increased 100 percent—but his taxes increased over 400 percent! His annual earnings of $20,000 catapulted him from the 16 percent tax bracket to the 24 percent tax bracket,[1] so that each year, $2,300 of his money went directly to the government. In addition, his Social Security contribution (actually a tax) had increased 248 percent. To make matters worse, no one could have foreseen the rate at which prices would soar, for while Henry's salary had doubled, the average price of consumer goods had *more than* doubled. For example, Henry had been paying $0.34 a gallon for gas to keep his Mustang running back in 1970; now he was paying an astounding $1.12 a gallon—an increase of 329 percent. Add to the picture, too, the fact that Henry's savings account, like a sitting duck, was

---

[1]See Appendix A for a full explanation of how tax brackets determine overall income tax. An understanding of this process is integral in making any investment decision.

accumulating only 5¼ percent interest while the annual inflation rate was well over double that rate. And as if his problems weren't bad enough, even his savings were threatened, for Henry had heard a rumor that the First National Savings Bank of Anytown was in financial trouble. Horrifying but true: Henry could lose it all. "So that's what they mean by 'safe as money in the bank,'" he thought bitterly. Who could blame Henry for feeling that he had somehow been betrayed?

There's Hope for Henry

Henry needn't give up hope, and neither should others who worked hard for their money and managed to set aside some of it over the years. But the old ways, it must be realized, no longer make sense. There is a way to get out from under. Henry doesn't realize it, but that camper can still be his. Moreover, with the right investments, he and his family can be assured of comfort in their later years as well as the gratification that comes with knowing you made the most of what you had.

The answer lies in making inflation—and the U.S. government—your business partner. While Henry bemoans the high prices and taxes that inflation created, he does not see that inflation is a two-sided coin: Sure, inflation is responsible for prices so high that no one could have predicted them, but inflation also enables Henry to earn as much as 15 percent annually on his savings. But in order to turn that coin over to its brighter side, Henry— and the rest of us—are going to have to start thinking a bit differently. It's called making inflation work for you. And make no mistakes about it: This cloud most definitely has a silver lining.

Our Changing Times

Economically, we are living today in a new environment in which the old rules, principles, and strategies are no longer applicable. Not only have things changed drastically, but they continue to change every day—without warning. Perhaps those people who deposited their money in 5¼ percent savings accounts had some idea that they could earn more for their dollars by investing elsewhere. What they did not know was that by *not* taking advantage of those other avenues, they were actually losing about 6 to 7 percent of their savings, since the inflation rate was more than double that 5¼ percent and, as if to complicate the matter, taxes were also being paid on those savings.

While all of the recommendations in this book address themselves to the new rules of the game, it is important first to understand the underlying principles on which they are based:

1. *Assume that inflation is here to stay.* Even if it levels off at, say, 7 percent over the next five years (and this is a very optimistic projection), that means that prices will double every ten years, and as we have seen in Henry's case, income usually does not rise proportionately to the inflation rate. The answer? Reduce taxable income through investments that will diminish—and in some cases eliminate —current taxes and defer gains until years later, when those profits will be taxed at a lower capital gains rate.[2]

2. *Learn how to make inflation work for you.* You can do this by taking advantage of the fact that those interest costs on loans, high as they are, are tax-deductible; by exploiting those opportunities that offer a return of 15 percent or better on your money; and by borrowing funds wisely to reinvest and earn more.

3. *Do not be fooled by the so-called safety of banks.* We know that the Federal Deposit Insurance Corporation (FDIC) and the Federal Savings and Loan Insurance Corporation (FSLIC) supposedly guarantee all bank deposits, but it has become increasingly obvious that these institu-

---

[2]Any investment that has been made over a period of more than one year falls into the capital gains category. Simply, this means that the IRS taxes its profit at less than one half the normal rate. It is through this method that the government is able to encourage long-term investments.

tions simply do not have enough funds to cover them all. In fact, at the end of 1981, the FSLIC had assets of only $6.8 billion, while it was conservatively estimated that the *failing* savings and loan associations had combined deposits of over $33 billion.[3] Thus this federal guarantee is obviously less than gilt-edged. Up to the present, the FDIC and the FSLIC have protected the smaller banks and savings and loan associations by merging them with larger ones. But this has been an expensive process and cannot go on indefinitely. On the other hand, the larger commercial banks in this country (Chase, Citicorp, Bank of America, etc.) are in financially sounder positions than their thrift institution cousins (savings banks and savings and loan associations). The federal government cannot let these behemoths ever cease to exist, for if they did, a worldwide crisis would result.

There is a way in which we can cope with the growing fallibility of banks, and the answer lies in learning the importance of investing only in the large institutions, meaning the big commercial banks and the big mutual funds, as we will discuss later on. Put your money in something that the government really cares about and you have made Uncle Sam your partner by letting him be your guarantor. Subsequent chapters in this book show you how.

4. *Start thinking the unthinkable*. It's more likely to occur than what you'd ordinarily expect. As in Henry's case, it was those people who were caught off guard—those who believed that life would most likely go on much as it had in the past—who made the biggest mistakes. What, then, is the unthinkable? It is the new rules of the game that will completely replace those old ways of thinking that were listed at the opening of this chapter. Let's reexamine them one more time.

> • *Keep your money in a bank; it's safest there*. As we've seen above, this couldn't be further from the

[3]Christian Hill and Paul A. Gigot, "Federal Regulators Are Said to Sanction Mergers Among Ailing Savings and Loans," *The Wall Street Journal*, February 18, 1982.

truth. Later on in this book we will show how money invested in the big mutual funds serves to safeguard savings while still keeping them accessible for living expenses.

- *Risks are for rich people.* Today risks are for everyone, for by taking no risk at all, it is most probable that you will lose. Obviously, there are different levels of risk, and these are reflected in the advice given in this book. One thing is for sure: Risk is very much part and parcel of the new rules of the economic game.

- *Don't borrow money; if you must, pay it off quickly.* If you believed this, you passed up the opportunity to get an 8½ percent thirty-year mortgage and have Uncle Sam paying for a good portion of the interest through tax benefits. That is, since interest payments are tax deductible, your taxable income would have been reduced, courtesy of the United States Government. Later on we will tell you how to borrow wisely to take advantage of these opportunities.

- *The best investments are U.S. savings bonds.* Today these bonds pay an interest rate of 7½ percent.[4] With inflation averaging over 10 percent during the past five years, it's easy to see that 7½ percent simply is not enough. And there is a better way. In fact, there are lots of them, and these are fully described in the chapters on mutual funds and government securities, which earn much better interest rates—at anywhere from 10 percent to 15 percent.

- *Never spend more than 25 percent of your annual income on housing.* Those people who are waiting for their incomes to increase to the point at which they will be able to comply with this rule are in for a surprise: Housing costs are rising much more rapidly than average incomes. The chances are that they'll never catch up. What's more, not only are

---

[4] They must be held for a minimum of five years to obtain a potentially higher return. See Chapter 6 for a full discussion of government securities.

mortgage rates skyrocketing, but it's probable that in the not-too-distant future, fixed-rate thirty-year mortgages will simply cease to exist. Instead, variable-rate mortgages whose interest rates will change annually will take their place. Chapter 8, however, deals with real-estate opportunities that *are* accessible to the small investor.

- *Social Security will take care of you when you retire.* It has been extensively reported that unless something drastic is done, Social Security funds will be completely depleted before this decade is over. The answer? Take advantage of the excellent opportunities that the Individual Retirement Act of 1981 offers. These are explained in Chapter 5, on IRAs.

Thinking the unthinkable does not end here, for a number of other new ideas must be fully realized as well in order to keep up with the current economic picture. For instance, did you always think that if you put your money in a money market fund that you'd be without cash in case of an emergency? It just isn't so. In fact, as the chapter on mutual funds illustrates, these investments are some of the most liquid available today. Did you think you had to be rich to be affected by taxes? Talk to Henry Jones about that one. Did you think you needed a lot of money to get involved in sound investments that would really make a difference in your life? The chapter on electric utility stocks will change your mind. Did you think you needed a B.A. in economics to understand anything beyond the simplest money matters? You'll think differently after reading this book.

And finally, did you think you didn't have $5,000 to invest? If so, read on.

2

How to Get $5,000—Instantly!

Five thousand dollars may seem like a lot of money, especially if you don't *have* $5,000, but consider this: It is quite possible that the money is there, somewhere among your present holdings and assets. Moreover, if this is the case, it is probable that the funds are more accessible to you than you imagined.

In the first part of this chapter I will attempt to assess your present financial status to ascertain whether your current income and assets, balanced against your current expenditures and debits, yield possible investment capital. Obviously, if we find that the funds are there, you need go no further. On the other hand, if they are not, you needn't worry: Sources of money are numerous, and later in this chapter I will explore a variety of them and evaluate which of these may be most wisely exploited.

Readers of this book who have suddenly come into windfalls of cash take note: Although you might already be in possession of the $5,000, this chapter is for you as well, for only by taking a close look at the finances in your life will you be best able to ascertain how much security you really have and which investments are best for you. Congratulations on that windfall—but read on!

Most people rarely take the time to learn about their financial worth, perhaps due to the obvious fear that the results will be somewhat depressing. However, it has been my experience that once my clients have overcome their initial worries about facing the music, they are often surprised and delighted with the song that ensues. But the importance of taking this step is twofold. You need to take a close look at your financial picture to determine how much investment capital you have (or don't have); beyond that, common sense tells us it is wise to find out where our money goes and to make intelligent choices about whether we'd like to continue those practices. Also remember that monthly savings are crucial to long-term profits if you are interested in supporting the investments you choose and in maximizing the profits. Only by examining your current cash-flow situation—your income and expenditures, that is—can areas of possible savings be identified.

With the help provided here, the tables that follow should be filled out honestly and realistically. As you execute these work sheets, remember that the resulting data will be only as accurate as the information you supply.

Your Personal Balance Sheet

To begin, take a look at your personal balance sheet on page 12, which addresses itself only to what you own and what you owe. (Income and spending will be dealt with further on.) The first part of Table 1 deals with current assets, or *what you own*.

Most people's largest asset is their home, if they own one (see line 1). Note that the table requires its current market value as opposed to what you paid for it or what you think you could get for it. The fastest, least expensive, and most accurate way to ascertain the present market value of your home is to consult the classified section of your local newspaper. Scan the "Homes for Sale" columns

Table 1.
Your Personal Balance Sheet

Assets (at current market value)

1. Home	$	_____
2. Automobile		_____
3. Cash surrender value of life insurance policies		_____
4. Checking account		_____
5. Savings account		_____
6. Money market funds		_____
7. Credit union accounts		_____
8. Stocks		_____
9. Bonds		_____
10. Mutual funds		_____
11. IRA/Keogh plans		_____
12. Collectibles		_____
13. Other assets		_____
Total assets	$	_____

Liabilities

14. Home mortgage	$	_____
15. Auto loan		_____
16. Credit card debt		_____
17. Retail charge account debt		_____
18. Other debts		_____
Total debts	$	_____
Personal financial net worth	$	_____
(total assets minus total debts)		

and jot down the prices of homes you are *sure* are similar to your own. These should be as close to your own home in size, age, condition, and, of course, location. For a truly accurate assessment, do this each week over a period of two or three weeks, then average those numbers (by adding them together and then dividing by the number of prices you have listed). Then reduce the final price by 10 percent. (Sorry, but those prices you copied down were the *asking* prices only and thus generally inflated.) Your final figure gives you a reasonable estimate of the current market value of your home. The chances are that that number is higher than what you expected.

12

Generally speaking, your second most valuable asset is probably your automobile. The most accurate way to ascertain its value is to consult the *Used Car Blue Book*, available in most libraries. On the other hand, you also can consult the classified ads in much the same way as you did for your home. Enter the number you get on line 2 of the balance sheet.

Line 3 refers to the cash surrender value of your life insurance policy, an especially important number to consider, since it is here that most people discover previously unrealized funds. These "pennies from heaven" will be discussed later in this chapter. For now, determine the current cash surrender value of your policy or policies either by consulting the policy itself or by querying your insurance agent directly. If you have a whole life, endowment, or straight life insurance policy, you will most likely discover a substantial cash surrender value—a real asset to be discussed later on. (Of course, borrowing against your cash surrender value does not jeopardize your policy; it does, however, mean that in case of your death, your beneficiary receives the face value of the policy *minus* the amount you have borrowed.)

Lines 4 and 5 of the balance sheet constitute the next step in filling out your list of assets, and these refer to both your checking and your savings accounts. These, together with any balances accumulated in money market funds (line 6) and credit union accounts [1] (line 7), represent your liquid assets, or assets that could be turned into cash almost immediately with very little risk. (Of course, if you are presently holding a substantial amount of cash, that should be included as well on line 13, for other assets.)

Next you must find out the current market value of any stocks, bonds, and mutual funds (lines 8, 9, and 10, respectively). Again, the key here is *current market value*, not what you paid for these. To find out *what you can sell*

---

[1] A credit union is a thrift institution usually affiliated with a labor union or large employer.

these for today, consult the agents, banks, or funds from which you purchased them. Remember, the fact that you may possibly have paid double the current price when you bought these years ago may be significant to you but not to their current market value.

IRA/Keogh plans (line 11) are next on your list of assets. Now and in the years ahead, these are the assets that will be building most rapidly. Later in this book you will find that Individual Retirement Accounts, or IRAs, are highly recommended to many different types of investors, and we will fully explain why. For present purposes, however, suffice it to say that while these are not considered liquid assets, they are assets nonetheless, and their value should be added and entered on line 11. Check your most recent annual statement to find out their values.

Collectibles (line 12) are another area of common assets that should not be overlooked. Quite often, in assessing their current financial worth, my clients have recalled their long-forgotten stamp or coin collections, started when they were children and now idly gathering dust in a dark attic. Many such collections are worth a great deal today. Whether or not you feel prepared to part with these, they constitute an important part of your financial picture, and their value should be assessed by the most reputable dealer you can locate. A special trip to a large metropolitan area may prove worthwhile, and you might even want to obtain comparative estimates. (If this is the course you choose, average the estimates and use that number.) Be sure your collection is insured before you leave it in the hands of a dealer; and I do urge you to seek out this sort of formal appraisal if you suspect that your collection is worth more than $1,000. If you're not sure, consult the appropriate references in your library.

Finally, the last line to be filled out in your assets list refers to any other holdings, such as jewelry, antique or fine furniture, trust accounts, and anything else you own that might be of significant value. Once again, estimate their current market value by consulting classified ads, pricing references, and reputable dealers.

You have now examined all of your assets. Add together the numbers you have entered in lines 1 to 13, enter the total on the line for your total assets, and set the sheet aside for the time being.

Take a deep breath.

The next step in filling out your balance sheet requires listing your liabilities, or what you owe. Most people know only too well how much money they owe at any given time, but bear in mind again that we're looking for the most accurate number we can come up with.

Start this list by ascertaining how much money is owed on your home mortgage, if you have one. Your annual mortgage statement, issued by the bank that holds your mortgage, shows the balance to be paid. Fill out line 14 on the balance sheet by entering the total amount of the principal due. Your statement will indicate principal as well as interest. (As you probably know, the money you repay in the first few years of that mortgage goes mostly toward paying off the interest due.)

Your next major liability probably is the repayment of an auto loan. Find out the balance due either by calling the bank from which the loan was made or by consulting your repayment coupon book. Enter the amount remaining on the loan on line 15.

Most people have some outstanding credit card debt or retail charge account balance (lines 16 and 17). If you're in this group, add these to your list of liabilities.

Finally, on line 18, add any outstanding debts you have, such as personal loans from friends or relatives, balances due on layaway plans, and even substantial bills that may not have been paid on time.

Now add together your total liabilities and then subtract that number from your total assets. The resulting number is an important one to remember, for it represents your personal financial net worth. That number tells you how much money you would have if you sold all your assets today and paid all your debts. It's likely that the number you have come up with is a bit higher than what you expected. This is the maximum amount of funds at your disposal today. Enter the number in the appropriate space on Table 1 and remember it, for you'll be working with it later in this chapter.

Table 2.
Your Personal Income Statement

Monthly Income

1. Wages, salaries, and bonuses	$_____
2. Interest income	_____
3. Dividend income	_____
4. Rental income	_____
5. Social Security income	_____
6. Private pension income	_____
7. Other income	_____
Total monthly income	$_____

Monthly Expenditures

8. Federal income tax	$_____
9. State and local taxes	_____
10. Social Security taxes	_____
11. Home mortgage payments	_____
12. Real-estate taxes	_____
13. Home or apartment rental	_____
14. Auto expenses	_____
15. Utilities (heating, phone, etc.)	_____
16. Food	_____
17. Clothing	_____
18. Medical care	_____
19. Insurance premiums	_____
20. Travel and entertainment	_____
21. Charitable contributions	_____
22. Other expenses	_____
Total monthly expenditures	$_____
Total monthly savings	$_____
(total monthly income minus total monthly expenditures)	

Filling out your personal income statement (see page 16) is the next step in assessing your financial worth and requires you to look at the actual sources and uses of your money. The numbers to be entered on this table represent *monthly* income and expenditures, so if you have access only to annual figures, remember to divide these by 12.

Start by entering your monthly wages, salaries, and bonuses (line 1). Work with gross amounts—that is, the amounts you take home before taxes, insurance payments, and union or Social Security contributions have been deducted.

Line 2 requires you to assess any interest income you might have from savings accounts, bonds, money market funds, or similar accounts. Check your latest statements to find out what these generally amount to on a monthly basis. If you find, when reviewing these figures, that your interest income from *low-yielding* bank accounts is high, trust that the rest of this book will help rectify that.

Dividend income (line 3) is paid on any stocks you might possess.

Rental income (line 4) refers to *net* income (that is, after all expenses are paid) from real estate you might be holding.

Lines 5 and 6 call for Social Security income, which, as of this writing, is usually tax-free; and private pension income, if any.

Finally, on line 7, add in any other monthly income you may have.

Now add lines 1 to 7 to arrive at your total monthly income.

Your monthly expenditures obviously are quite critical to understanding your spending patterns, for no matter how much you earn, what you spend each month can easily eat up that lofty income.

The first line on your list of monthly expenditures (line 8) represents Uncle Sam's share of your pie, which unfortunately is likely to be quite a slice. Check your most recent tax statement to ascertain your annual taxes. (Here and throughout the rest of this list, be sure to divide by 12 when dealing with annual sums.)

Next, enter your state and local taxes (line 9) and then your Social Security contribution (line 10).[2]

If you own a home, you invariably have a monthly mortgage payment (line 11), unless you were so fortunate as to have paid off the entire amount at those beautiful 5 to 6 percent mortgage rates of yesteryear. Enter your real estate taxes on line 12.

If you do not own a home, enter your monthly home or apartment rental expenses on line 13.

The remaining monthly expenses should be fairly simple to figure out. Again, try to be honest about what you actually spend on the items listed on lines 14 to 22, making sure you've included *all* your "guilty pleasures." If you know that your entertainment expenditures are exorbitant, face it; you really do need to know where your money is going.

While I'll leave you on your own to assess these last expenses, I would like to add a word here on auto expenses. The average cost of running a fairly used car is $0.22 per mile; for a new car, the cost is $0.38 per mile—and these amounts are rising annually with the increasing costs of automobiles and gasoline. Thus, if you drive your new car an average of twelve thousand miles per year, your total annual cost is $4,560, or $380 monthly. This excludes parking fees, tolls, and fines for parking or moving violations. Enough said; these statistics should start you thinking.

Now add your total monthly expenditures and then subtract this number from your total monthly income to arrive at your total monthly savings. Hopefully this will be a positive number, and if that is the case, you now know how much money you have available to you on a monthly basis for investing. On the other hand, if you arrive at a

---

[2]Note that while Social Security payments commonly are called contributions, they are actually a tax of sorts but are not tax-deductible, as state and local taxes are.

18

negative number, the fact is that you spend more money than you earn; and let's face it, you cannot continue this practice indefinitely. There are, of course, ways to remedy the situation. You can reduce your spending habits, get a second job to increase your income, find higher-yielding investments, or reduce your taxes. While these latter two approaches will be emphasized throughout this book, some personal belt-tightening may be in order as well. Think about it, and discuss the possibilities with the other culprits in your family.

You have now realistically determined both your financial net worth and your annual savings rate (multiply the monthly sum by 12 to arrive at the annual total), and you have two very important pieces of information you didn't have before. The annual savings rate tells you how much money you presently have on hand for investing and ultimately ensuring a sound financial future. If the annual sum amounts to $5,000 or more, you're really ready for the next chapter.

Your financial net worth, on the other hand, tells you the maximum amount you would have to invest if you were to sell all you own and reinvest the proceeds in other ways. However, most people are not willing to take this drastic step, and we hardly expect you to. The point of preparing the statement was actually to get you to take a better look at the current value of your assets and to find out where your funds have been placed. Later on in this chapter we will ask you to think about them further.

What to Do Even If You Don't Have $5,000

As I've promised, there are ways to obtain $5,000 if your annual savings rate indicates you don't have the cash you need. Consider the sources that follow, paying special attention to the advantages and consequences of each. Somewhere among them $5,000 await you.

Cash surrender on life insurance policies is the source of money that most people do not realize they have at their disposal. Your life insurance policy is possibly worth money— maybe lots of it—and the best part is, you don't have to die for it to be available.

As we have mentioned previously, if you have a whole life, endowment, or straight life insurance policy, you probably qualify for these funds, and if you purchased your policy ten to twenty years ago, it probably was one of those types. (Term insurance policies do not offer cash surrender values.) If this is the case, you could easily have $2,000, $5,000, or even $10,000 cash surrender on your policy. The most remarkable aspect of all this is that you probably can borrow up to 95 percent of the amount at the incredibly low interest rate of either 5 or 6 percent—without jeopardizing your policy.

If you have followed the suggestions on page 13 for determining the cash surrender value of your policy, then you already know whether such a bonanza awaits you. Check the policy again; it should also state the percentage at which you can borrow against the sum.

To find out the present worth of the policy and to arrange to get your hands on the cash, you will probably have to call your insurance agent or the company that issued the policy. It's likely they will try to dissuade you from making the loan. Be persistent; remember that the money is yours.

If you do decide to borrow against the policy (and this source of funds is certainly recommended if you have it at your disposal), you may repay the loan as quickly or as slowly as you desire. It is strongly advised that you stay current on the interest payments at least; if you don't, the value of your policy may be reduced. If you die before the loan is repaid, the face value of the policy is reduced by the amount of money you still owed.

At this point in your quest for funds you might be wise to review your life insurance needs to find out whether you are carrying too much insurance. Chapter 7 offers step-by-step instructions for evaluating these needs in the section titled "Who Needs Life Insurance?" If you follow the guidelines there and find that you've been wasting money annually on unnecessary premiums, by all means cash in that policy, or the excess portion of it, and consider the extra money as part—or all—of your investment capital.

Borrowing Against Your Pension Plan Funds

This is another often-overlooked source of funds. You may have completely forgotten that your employer issues this plan, or you may simply be unaware of the fact that often you can borrow against it. Many pension funds, especially the contributory type (that is, where the employer as well as the employee contribute toward the fund), offer borrowing privileges, and again, the interest rates on these "loans" are quite reasonable—usually 7 or 8 percent. Obviously, the amount you can borrow depends on the amount you have contributed to the fund and on the number of years you have participated in it. Generally, you can borrow approximately 80 to 90 percent of the accumulated value. For reasons that should now be apparent, how these funds work and how they may be borrowed against are not very well publicized by pension plan administrators. But bear in mind that the money is yours and that this one source may very well yield the $5,000 needed for the investment strategies I detail later. Remember to be inquisitive, persistent, and resourceful; no one else can do that for you.

To determine whether you can borrow against your pension plan fund, contact the personnel department at your place of employment or your employer's benefits coordinator. The information should be readily obtainable. You may work out a schedule for repaying only the interest on the loan, or the interest and the principal. But the principal does not have to be repaid. My advice is to pay the interest and wisely invest the rest. Remember, though, that upon retirement or death, the borrowed sums, if they have not been repaid, are subtracted from your pension proceeds.

Your Personal Savings Account

Are you one of those people who contributed toward the $340 billion that was sitting in 5½ percent savings accounts in 1982?

I wish I had a dollar for every raised eyebrow I've encountered when I've suggested to people that they use their personal savings for investment purposes. As I've told my clients and as you will learn in the next chapter, those savings can be earning you considerably more than the 5 to 5½ percent in interest they are presently gathering. Consider also that that meager interest rate is fully taxable, so that what you really wind up with is a lot closer to, say, 3 percent after taxes. As you read on, you will find that it is entirely possible to double or even triple the rate of interest earned on your savings; and as these methods come to light, you will realize that even with an optimistic outlook toward inflation, savings accounts are, to put it mildly, a poor investment practice.

To be sure, it is important to keep that money liquid, or available and very safe. And this can be done, often within the very same bank that currently holds your account—but with double the rate of return.

The point is, if you have more than $500 in a low-interest savings account, it is imperative for you to consider that money as part of your investment capital. And if this is the case, you will do yourself a great service by reading the rest of this book quickly and implementing the investment programs recommended immediately so you do not lose another day's interest.

My approach to the credit cards I hold is quite different from that of most people, for I view these not as vehicles for charging purchases but as personal lines of credit—as instant loans, if you will. And while I am not even going to suggest here that these funds be viewed as investment capital, they are worth discussing here for this reason: Credit card lines offer security in that they make money available to you in time of need. So whereas you might have kept, say, $3,000 in your savings account at all times in case of emergency, you can regard a credit line as your emergency fund while putting those savings to work for you instead.

MasterCard and Visa, to name just two, offer credit lines of anywhere from $500 to $20,000, depending on many factors, most notably your income. It is common for businesses and large corporations always to have available lines of credit, and they pay for these whether or not they are used. On the other hand, you as an individual may very likely qualify for a substantial credit line of $2,000, $3,000, or even $5,000 for an annual fee as low as $15—tax-deductible, no less—or even for no fee at all. (See Appendix C for a list of thirteen major banks across the country that offer credit lines on a no-fee or low-fee basis.)

While this available cash can be seen as a true windfall—and I do suggest you take advantage of it as your needs predict—let me caution you: Once you use that money, you are at the mercy of their substantial interest rates—rates that are even higher than the expected yields on the very best investments. For this reason, I do not recommend that this money be used for investment purposes. Nevertheless, the credit is valuable to you in that the security it offers you may free other funds to be used more advantageously.

Even if you don't imagine that you will ever take advantage of this source of money, remember that the hardest times to get your hands on cash is when you need it the most; at those times your free credit line can be a real life-saver.

Although I have already covered the major sources of money available to you, my clients usually discover that they can come up with even more if they look hard enough. Think hard about whether you are holding assets that can possibly be more productive to you.

This is a good time to review the list of assets you prepared earlier. If you own a second car, think about how often you really use it. Remember that in addition to the cash to be derived from its sale, you'll also increase your monthly savings by the amount it costs you to run that car and by the cost of the insurance policy you've been paying. Even a ten-year-old car, in good running condition, can fetch as much as $1,000 in today's marketplace.

How about that stamp or coin collection you might have overlooked? Does its nostalgic value really outweigh the income it might produce? What about old jewelry that might have lost its glitter? Is it worth anything? A trip to a reputable appraiser can be a real eye-opener.

Examine the bonds you might be holding; if you are earning in the neighborhood of 8 percent or less, it probably makes sense to sell them, for you'll find that we can easily put those funds to better use.

Finally, take a look around your home—especially the attic—for furniture and household items that are doing little more than taking up space. They may not seem to be worth a lot, but put them together—along with any old clothing, toys your children have outgrown, old books and records, the fishing rod you haven't touched in years—and you have the goods for a garage sale that might take in from $500 to $1,000. You'll be surprised at how resourceful you can be when the motivation is there. And bear in mind that the rewards to be had from your investments are more than just food for thought. Remember, too, that every little bit helps.

Happy hunting!

How Not to Get $5,000

There are two sources of funds I do not recommend, and I would like to discuss them here briefly.

The first involves borrowing from finance companies, and the reasons to steer away from these should be quite obvious: Their interest rates simply are too high. Remember that the cost of the money you invest should never be higher than the interest to be derived from your investments. It was precisely for this reason that I recommended *not* using credit card lines for investment capital.

The second source of money to stay away from involves taking out a second mortgage on your home, and there are several reasons for my negative feelings about this.

Your home, if you own one, is your greatest source of collateral and therefore probably your greatest asset. I feel, then, that as such it should be saved as a last resort, as in a real life-or-death situation, or in case you decide to alter your life drastically by starting a new career or even opening a new business. The house you own is more valuable as collateral than the money to be acquired from a second mortgage, especially since those funds would be reinvested. Of course, a second mortgage could yield an enormous amount of money, but I feel that it should be saved for the most appropriate time and situation. Remember, too, that if you were to take out a second mortgage, you would have to pay a hefty interest rate on the money you borrowed, and the repayment plan would involve the kind of long-term commitment that is probably not warranted.

You have come a long way in this chapter. You have assessed your financial worth, and you have taken a close, honest look at the money in your life and how you spend it. If you are like the men and women I have advised, you probably have discovered a few things about your financial habits that you are not too proud of. But it's never too late to learn about yourself and to make necessary changes. The fact that you have been this honest with yourself indicates that you have taken that first, very important step. Hopefully you have also found that things are not really as bad as they seemed and that you have more going for you than you previously imagined.

Happily, these surprises are just the beginning.

3

How to Invest up to $5,000

You are now ready to examine the investment programs I
recommend for each of four types of investors. Before you
choose, I urge you to read through the entire chapter to
determine which program comes closest to meeting your
needs, for as you'll see, situations can vary enormously,
and while one program may offer considerably higher
profits, there are certain give-and-take factors to be noted.
For instance, some programs address themselves to individuals who can afford to make long-term investments,
since their current living expenses are relatively low. Another program might offer low percentages while keeping
funds more liquid for the needs of a growing family; these
would be shorter-term investments. Again, review each of
the categories before you decide, "That's me!"

Finally, a word of caution regarding the investment
capital you've located. Before you embark on any program,
make certain you have enough funds to cover your present
living needs, for I have never meant to imply that investing is more important than living. While I have shown, in
the last chapter, that a hefty savings account might be put
to better use, you should know that it would be foolish *not*
to have a sum set aside for emergencies, because any

investment involves risks and you must be ready and able to get by if you lose. Lines of credit, as I've mentioned, can partially fill this need.

In addition, especially if you're in the process of starting or raising a family, or if you are self-employed, be sure that your health needs are adequately covered by a comprehensive health insurance program. Unfortunately, the best health coverage generally is available only to large employer groups. Get the most comprehensive health insurance you can comfortably afford. To make this a little more affordable, look for a $250 or even a $500 family annual deductible, which could mean substantial savings on premiums.[1] Review your health insurance program to ascertain whether you have adequate coverage.

Finally, bear in mind that if you haven't been able to extract $5,000 from your personal financial analysis, note that all of the following programs, except for the last, are broken down into smaller increments that you may be able to afford. Thus, if you find that you are a member of Group A and have only $2,000 to invest, it would make sense to follow only the first point in that program.

Group A

This group consists primarily of single or married people under thirty-five who have no children and are in a relatively high tax bracket due to a lack of deductions and exemptions (they own no real estate, have few dependents, etc.). These are the investors who can afford to take the highest risks, since their financial responsibilities are largely limited and they require the least amount of liquidity. Since this group is not overly concerned with current investment income, their program is designed to yield

---

[1]The higher the deductible, the lower the annual premiums. For example, if you could afford a $1,000 family deductible, this could cut your premium cost 30 to 50 percent.

maximum profits over a longer period. The recommendations prescribed for Group A follow.

- $2,000 to be invested in IRA funds, broken down into two sums: For instance, $1,000 in a high-risk aggressive growth mutual fund (at an expected annual return of 15 to 20 percent); and $1,000 to be placed in a money market mutual fund (at an expected return rate of 10 to 14 percent).[2] Since the former of these is a bit more risky than the latter, dividing the capital in this way offers the investor a hedge toward a more moderate risk. Furthermore, Chapter 5 explains how to make additional choices regarding the breakdown of your IRA funds. While placing $1,000 in either of these funds certainly will result in a handsome profit, we recommend, in the case of this particular investment, that $1,000 be placed in them *annually*. Table 1 gives some idea of just how attractive those returns can be when this program is undertaken on an ongoing basis. For

Table 1.
Total Profits Accruing from $1,000
Invested in an IRA Fund at Various Rates
Each Year for Ten Years

Rate of Return	Total Capital Accumulated	Total Profit
12%	$19,700	$ 9,700
15%	23,350	13,350
20%	31,150	21,150

[2]If both spouses work, the amount of money placed in an IRA fund may be doubled, to $4,000. If this is the case, follow the recommendation given here, placing half the money in the high-risk aggressive growth mutual fund and half in the money market mutual fund.

complete information on the possible risks and rewards of investing in mutual funds, see Chapter 4.

- $1,000 to be used to purchase three gold coins when gold is selling for $300 an ounce or less. These are to be sold when gold reaches $500 an ounce at a profit of 66⅔ percent (or approximately $600). This profit will be further enhanced by the fact that it probably will fall into the category of capital gains and therefore will be taxed at a lower rate. Chapter 8 explains how and why gold prices fluctuate and how to plan this investment.

- $2,000 to be distributed in the following manner: $1,000 in a money market mutual fund for safety of principal and moderate rate of return; and $1,000 in an aggressive growth mutual fund for potentially high long-term rates of return. By purchasing both the money market and aggressive growth mutual funds from the same family of funds, you may switch your investment between these two at no charge. Chapter 4 discusses these families of funds and explains the advantages of no-load, or no-charge, fund purchases.

Group B

This group includes married couples under forty who have children. Although there are possibly two wage earners in this family, they are most likely to have the greatest financial responsibilities (such as housing and the costs of raising children) with the least resources available to meet them. Their concerns about the future are great, since they anticipate the high costs of college education for their youngsters while they are also concerned about estate planning for their later years. Because the purchase of real estate can play an extremely important role in the lives of Group B members and because there are a great number of profitable opportunities in this area, the Group B plan has been broken down for two groups: those who already own their own homes and those who do not.

30

Plan I (for nonhomeowners)

- $150 for the first annual premium toward the purchase of a $100,000 term life insurance policy. This is the cheapest insurance available and the most crucial investment for Group B members, since it establishes an automatic estate. This investment should be regarded as mandatory; in fact, it is so important that we have taken the liberty of extending the investment packages for Group B to a total of $5,150. Chapter 9, which describes the variety of insurance programs available and offers specific recommendations, explains the necessity of this investment—and the hazards of overlooking it—more fully.

- $5,000 to be used to purchase a house, cooperative, or condominium. The tax advantages of this investment are so substantial that it is set forth as a "must" here if the prospective investor does not already own a home. But there are a number of realities to be faced here: If Group B members follow Plan I and have no access to additional funds, they must realize that they are sacrificing liquidity of funds. Therefore we suggest that these investors be amply covered by a comprehensive health insurance program in case of emergency and that they refer to Chapter 2 to obtain no-fee or low-fee credit cards and the credit lines these offer for additional emergency funds. Furthermore, although it is possible to purchase a home for as little as $5,000 down (Chapter 8 shows how this may be done through seller financing and other creative devices), buyers must realize that monthly mortgage payments may be substantial. So while things may be "tight" for a while, the tax advantages to be had will make those sacrifices worthwhile. We strongly suspect that investors will look back on this purchase one day viewing it as the wisest one ever made.

31

Plan II (for homeowners)

- $150 toward the purchase of a $100,000 term life insurance policy (see page 94).
- $2,000 to be invested in IRA plans, broken down into two sums; for instance, $1,000 in a long-term growth mutual fund (at an expected annual return of 15 percent); and $1,000 in a money market mutual fund (at an expected annual return of 10 to 14 percent). Chapter 5 explains other possible breakdown choices. As we have seen in the prescribed program for Group A, splitting the funds in this way helps the investor to maintain a more moderate risk while still enjoying the highest possible return rates.
- $3,000 to be placed in a money market mutual fund, guaranteeing relative safety at an expected annual return rate of 10 to 14 percent and a high degree of liquidity. (In fact, these may actually be thought of and utilized as high-interest checking accounts.) The differences among the many different types of mutual funds and their treatment by the IRS under various conditions are explained in Chapter 4.

Group C

Typical Group C investors would be single persons or married couples in their middle years. If these people had children, they are probably grown by now and on their own. For Group C members, it is probably a time of greatest income relative to their responsibilities. If mortgages are not entirely paid off by now, the chances are that few payments are remaining. Group C members have reached what is possibly going to be their highest level of earning, especially since, in the case of married couples, they are possibly living on two incomes now. Their investment program reflects greater concern for retirement planning than it does for current income; thus, the object of their strategy is to defer taxable income on investments until after age sixty-five, when they will be taxed at a much lower rate. Group C is offered the following investment portfolio:

- $2,000 (or $4,000 in the case of married couples in which both spouses are working)[3] to be placed in IRA accounts, broken down as follows: half the money in a money market mutual fund offering an expected annual return of 10 to 14 percent, and half into life insurance investments—but only if it is possible to obtain a policy that guarantees a fixed interest rate of 12 to 14 percent or higher over a six-year period. If such a policy is not obtainable, then all of the funds are to be placed in the money market mutual fund described above. Again, dividing the investment in this way ensures a relatively high return and a good degree of safety. The strong advantage of IRA insurance fund investments, as they are called, is the possible *fixed* rate of return.

- $3,000 to be invested in electric utility stocks, which offer an expected annual rate of return between 12 and 17 percent. Under the Economic Recovery Act of 1981, utility stocks have become very favorable tax considerations: Investors are now allowed to reinvest dividends in additional stocks without paying taxes on up to $750 of these per year ($1,500 on a joint return). Once the newly acquired shares are sold, the income on them will be taxed at a much more favorable long-term capital gains rate, provided they have been held for at least one year. This situation provides the investor with the ability to defer current taxes and substantially reduce them in the future. But the most important aspect of this investment will be the correct selection of the util-

---

[3]If $4,000 is invested in IRAs, then Group C investors are to invest only the remaining portion of their $5,000 ($1,000) in the electric utility stocks, which are described immediately below.

- ity stock itself; Chapter 10 will make specific suggestions and describe the transactions fully.

Group D

Group D consists of retired persons who find themselves in the position of being able to take the least amount of risk, for their priority now is for higher (and safer) current income. Generally speaking, income tax is not a significant consideration in the investment decisions that Group D members make, since their age, if they are over sixty-five, entitles them to a more favorable tax situation. Their program, then, is designed to yield a relatively fast turnover of profits within a short period of time. Here are the best investments for this group:

- $5,000 to be placed in a two-year treasury notes for a 12 to 15 percent annual return, nontaxable by municipalities and states, although federal taxes still will be due. These treasury notes may be purchased directly from the Federal Reserve System through any one of their twelve Federal Reserve banks (which are listed in Chapter 6) at no handling charge. This is one of the safest—although somewhat less liquid—investments around, since the U.S. government is directly obligated to it.

Note: If Group D investors started out with as much as $10,000 to invest, they are to disregard the above recommendation and instead purchase six-month or one-year treasury bills, which are also issued through the Federal Reserve. These funds are the safest in the world today, but they do require a minimum cash outlay of $10,000.[4] They can automatically be renewed every six months (or yearly) at no extra cost to the investor, and their rate of

---

[4]Furthermore, they can be purchased only in $5,000 increments after the initial $10,000 investment is made.

return has been between 9 and 15 percent, which, again, is not subject to municipal or state tax.

Now that you have reviewed the programs and discovered which one is right for you, refer to subsequent chapters of this book for complete instructions on how to implement the various points in the programs. But rather than having you turn to just those chapters that address your specific program, I strongly urge you to read through this book in its entirety, for each of its sections contains highly useful pieces of information that, taken together, explain just how the financial aspects of our society operate. Whether or not government securities are on your list of investments, Chapter 6 explains how banks work and when they're likely to fail. The discussion on IRAs offers further insight into the subject. And, you'll find, almost every chapter deals with a bit of economic history that is useful and relevant to all of us.

4

Mutual Funds

You have noted, in the preceding chapter, that mutual funds were recommended to a number of different types of investors; this chapter is intended for the readers in those categories. But even if mutual funds are not on your prescribed list of investments, I urge you to read on: There's useful information here for anyone interested in a better understanding of the opportunities available in today's market, and mutual funds might interest you in the future if your situation changes.

Although there are many different types of mutual funds available on the market today, I recommended only three in the previous chapter: money market funds, growth stock funds, and (aggressive growth) maximum capital gains funds. In this chapter I will explore the advantages of these and will show you how to participate in them and subsequently take advantage of what I feel is one of the most exciting options available to small investors today.

What They Are and How They Work

Mutual funds, or open-end investment companies, as they are officially known, have been in their present form for over forty years, having been established by the Investment Company Act of 1940. As of August 1983, there were over 690 different mutual funds in existence, with dozens of different investment objectives. Generally speaking, these companies pool resources collectively from thousands or even millions of investors for a particular investment objective; they accomplish this goal by investing your money in a number of places. The funds—and the investment choices to be made—are handled by full-time professional investment managers who probably can do better than the average individual.

The various types of mutual funds are defined by their objectives. Thus, *growth stock funds* invest their money in the stock of leading growth companies that have performed well over a long period; *maximum capital gains funds*, or aggressive growth funds, invest in the stock of smaller, newer companies that the funds feel have the greatest capital gains, or long-term, potential; and *money market funds* invest money in money market instruments, such as treasury bills, commercial paper, and certificates of deposit. These three types of funds will be discussed in greater detail below, and as we learn about how they work, you will see why these three were specifically and solely recommended.

Briefly, the mechanics of mutual funds work as follows: When you purchase shares of a mutual fund, you pay the *net asset value*, or NAV, per share; that is the net worth of the portfolio on the day you bought it divided by the outstanding number of shares. When you choose to sell your shares, the fund must, by law, buy them from you at the NAV of the shares. This aspect of mutual funds constitutes their main advantage: guaranteed marketability, which we will examine further later on.

Dividends and interest received by the funds on the investments they have made are distributed to shareholders quarterly, except in the case of money market funds, which pass on their profits daily. Many investors find it advantageous and convenient to have their dividends and interest reinvested in the fund automatically, especially where money market profits are concerned.

Similarly, when funds sell some of their investments, the net capital gains, or profits, are passed on to shareholders.

All mutual funds charge an annual management fee of roughly ½ percent of net assets. In addition, some funds impose a sales charge, or load, as it is called—usually 8½ percent of the money invested. It's easy to see the disadvantage here: Your fund has to earn 8½ percent before you can break even. The funds that charge this sales fee are called *load funds*. However, there are *no-load* funds as well—those that require no sales fees or which charge only minimal ones (1 to 2 percent); while these have existed for many years, it is only in the past half decade or so that they have come to dominate the market. In fact, while 80 percent of all mutual funds available ten years ago were of the load variety, that statistic is now reversed: Today 80 percent of existing mutual funds, in addition to most new ones that appear on the market regularly, are *no-loads*. You'll be happy to find, then, that the three types of mutual funds I have recommended are all no-load funds. Later I will make specific recommendations as to which of these you are better off investing in, but you might also want to obtain a complete list of all no-load mutual funds, which also lists their respective services, minimum investment requirements, and investment objectives as well as addresses and phone numbers. For this information, write to: No-Load Mutual Fund Association, Valley Forge Colony Building, Valley Forge, PA 19481.

Before we leave the subject of loads vs. no-loads, I would like to make one more important point: Please do not let anyone try to convince you that loads have anything to do with the performance of a fund. There are some great load funds and some lousy ones as well; the same is true for no-loads. Be aware that at some point in your life a broker might try to tell you that an 8½ percent charge will ensure you a greater profit. He will say, "You get what you pay for," but it's just not true in this case.

Up until recently, mutual funds were tied closely to the

fortunes of the stock market, since most funds invested in stocks. This was fine for a while, since in the mid-to-late sixties, the stock market did quite well. In fact, in the latter part of that decade, high-performance mutual funds, then called go-go funds, were all the rage. At that time, mutual funds in general and these go-go funds in particular promised—regardless of the realism of these promises— consistently high rates of return almost regardless of the stock market climate. During much of the 1966–68 period the go-go funds delivered, yielding 50 percent and higher returns annually.[1] However, during the 1969–70 stock market slump, the inevitable happened, and these funds found themselves suffering losses of 50 to 90 percent. If you know anything at all about the history of mutual funds, you probably heard that they were terribly unpopular during the 1970s; it was this sharp debacle of these highly publicized mutual funds that was responsible, for the adverse effect that the decline had on the industry was to last for almost a decade. In fact, it is only during the last three to four years that the mutual fund industry has come back into favor, and today it is enjoying a healthy renaissance. The savior proved to be the highly successful money market funds. The money market funds, which are no-load, became so popular and advantageous that the public gave a second and favorable look at mutual funds in general. Thus, the goodwill developed by the money market funds helped the entire industry. In turn, the industry finally realized that the main selling point of mutual funds was that they alone could give the small investor a diversified portfolio of stocks, bonds, and money market instruments for an initial investment as low as $1,000, something that is almost impossible to do outside mutual funds.

---

[1]For an interesting discussion of these funds and those years, see John Brook's *The Go-Go Years* (New York: Weybright and Talley), 1973.

The Advantages of Investing in Mutual Funds

It's almost impossible to define mutual funds without talking about some of their advantages, and the chances are that you already can guess a few of them. From a technical standpoint, however, the primary reasons for investing in them center on the fact that you get a great *diversification of investments at reduced risk* while being assured of constant *marketability* for what you have purchased while enjoying the constant services of *professional management*.

Diversification

Diversification of investments at reduced risk is by far the most important factor in mutual fund investing. This aspect is sometimes called spreading the risk, but that's a misnomer; actually, what you're doing is *reducing* the risk.

If you were to start with, say, $1,000 or $2,000 as investment capital, you could buy a substantial amount of stock in only one or two companies. Say one of these companies failed—and, to make matters worse, the failure could not possibly have been foreseen, for your poor judgment was not to blame; rather, it was an uncontrollable circumstance, of a type such as 1982's Tylenol disaster. You would have lost a significant portion of your investment. On the other hand, had you invested that money in a mutual fund, your money would have been reinvested in a diversified portfolio, say, twenty different stocks. The damage done by that one poor performer, then, probably would have been offset by the nineteen other stocks.

Mutual funds, then, allow you to participate in a broad range of investments you probably could not afford on your own, and you reduce the risk involved while still having the same potential rate of return.

Marketability

Marketability ensures you a ready buyer for your mutual fund shares *whenever you are ready to sell them,* for the fund must, by law, buy them back at the NAV whenever you choose. This is of critical importance, especially in view of what I predict will be an extremely volatile market in the years ahead.

You will be better able to appreciate this aspect of mutual funds if you ever purchased an over-the-counter stock and later tried to sell it in what had become a slumping market. It was very possible that no one wanted to buy your stock, and you were stuck. Not so with mutual funds.

Professional Management

Mutual funds charge annual management fees that usually amount to ½ percent of your total investment; thus, if you were to invest $5,000 in a fund, the charge would be $25. It's minimal, as you can see, and in my opinion, well worth the money. Not that the people who manage the fund are necessarily geniuses or even, for that matter, smarter than you. But they are full-time professionals who have access to a multitude of information that nonprofessionals probably wouldn't have time to read even if they did get their hands on it. The fallacy that individuals can choose stocks and monitor them and diversify them as well is, I think, the main reason why most people lose money in the stock market.

And Another Thing . . .

Another advantage of investing in mutual funds (and especially in only the largest ones, which is what I advise) is that you can often shift your investments, often with no sales charge, from one group of investments to as many as

41

ten others within the same mutual fund group. For example, a fund such as Dreyfus offers many different investment funds, such as their Liquid Asset Fund, their Special Income Fund, and their Third-Century Fund, to name just a few. The fact that you can switch from one to the other will be especially helpful to you as you learn to take advantage of the ever-changing financial and economic environment.

The funds that appear on the following list are all *families* of funds that offer no-loads primarily. If you invest in one of these and decide to switch after a time, you can transfer your money to another fund within the same larger family, usually without even having to pay an additional service fee.

Later in this chapter I will explain how to obtain investment applications from these companies and make your initial investment.

Seven Mutual Fund Family Groups That Offer Primarily No-Load Funds

Value Line
711 Third Avenue
New York, NY 10017
(212)687-3965
(800)223-0828
Offers six different no-load funds

Fidelity Group
82 Devonshire Street
Boston, MA 02109
(617)523-1919
(800)225-6190
Offers twenty-two different no-load funds

Alliance/Wood Struthers
140 Broadway
New York, NY 10008
(212)269-1500
(800)221-7780
Offers five different no-load funds

Scudder Funds
174 Federal Street
Boston, MA
(617)482-3990
(800)225-2470
Offers ten different no-load funds

Dreyfus Group
767 Fifth Avenue
New York, NY 10153
(212)895-1206
(800)223-5525
*Offers eight different no-load funds in addition to the Dreyfus Leverage Fund, which is a load fund and therefore not recommended**

T. Rowe Price Funds
100 East Pratt Street
Baltimore, MD 21202
(301)547-2308
(800)638-1527
Offers eight different no-load funds

Vanguard Group
P.O. Box 2600
Valley Forge, PA 19482
(215)648-6000
(800)523-7025
Offers twenty-two different no-load funds

The Disadvantages of Mutual Funds

Frankly, there aren't many.

One possible disadvantage of investing in mutual funds is that you lack control over your specific investment purchase. For example, if the fund you went with decided to invest a portion of your money in the firm that manufactured Rely tampons in 1981, when that company had more than its share of disasters, you were stuck. But this loss would have been offset in a number of ways. In the first place, the other investments the fund chose probably would have minimized the loss in that one area, making the effect on your overall investment small. In the second place, as we've mentioned, each fund starts out with a specific goal in mind. Had you disapproved of that goal, you would not have found yourself investing in that fund. Third (and again, this point has been made), you do have the option of switching from one fund to another within a family of funds. Thus the flexibility of your investment comes into play.

---

*In 1983 the Dreyfus Fund became a no-load fund for investments above $500.

43

The only other disadvantage I can see in mutual funds is that they all charge a management fee. But as I've said, this ½ percent per year is money well spent, given the advantages I've pointed out. Bear in mind that if you wanted to—and could afford to—use the services of a personal investment adviser, the fee would be substantially greater than ½ percent a year.

Money Market Mutual Funds

As I've noted elsewhere, the money market funds helped the mutual fund industry regain its vibrancy after the 1969–70 stock market slump. For the small investor, money market funds have become an extremely viable investment vehicle, for they offer relatively high rates of return with relatively small amounts of risk, which can be reduced further by taking a few precautions I will explain below.

A money market fund actually acts as a loan company, in a sense, extending credit and funds, primarily on a short-term basis (less than ninety days), to the U.S. government, commercial banks, and major corporations. Were you to purchase U.S. treasury bills, for example, you would be doing the same thing—lending your money to the government—as the money market mutual fund. But the trouble is that such investments usually are not accessible to the small investor, since the minimum cost of a treasury bill is $10,000; the minimum short-term obligation to major corporations, called *commercial paper*, is $25,000; and the short-term obligations of large commercial banks, called *certificates of deposit*, usually start at $100,000. But the money market fund, pooling the capital of all its investors, can and does purchase these treasury bills, certificates of deposit, and commercial paper, enabling you to take advantage of interest rates that would not be available to you otherwise. For all you need to get started in a money market fund is a minimum of usually $1,000.

Money market mutual funds were started in 1971 with the Reserve Fund. By 1974, there were nineteen money market funds in existence with combined assets of less than $3 billion. And my, how they've grown: By October 1982 there were 211 taxable money market funds with combined assets of an astronomical $225.9 billion.[2]

Obviously, in order to achieve this sort of phenomenal growth in ten short years, they must have been providing some fairly useful investment services to their clients, and their history points to the fact that they have indeed done so. These funds provided a vehicle that gave investors up to 16 percent interest during the 1981–82 period; in the years before that, the average rates of return were between 10 and 14 percent—still respectable, especially if you examine those rates in light of the 5½ percent that banks were paying on savings accounts. No wonder, then, that many savings banks and savings and loan companies lost so many of their depositors to money market funds.

The obvious advantage of money market funds is the relatively high rates of return they offer. They also feature a high degree of liquidity (your money is available to you when you need it) and low risk, although the funds are not guaranteed by the FDIC or any other government agency, a point we'll examine in a moment. The interest you accrue in a money market fund is compounded daily. Furthermore, most funds issue "checkbooks" upon request, and these can be used to write checks for $500 or more. Thus you may use this account as a high-interest-bearing checking account. When the check is received by the fund, it becomes an automatic withdrawal, and interest is paid on that money right up until the day the check clears. Pretty nifty, huh?

Of course, there are some disadvantages, the main one being that the funds are not protected by FDIC insurance or by any other government agency, whereas money in the bank is. But since the money market funds invest only in the highest-quality financial instruments, the risk can

---

[2]*Barron's*, October 25, 1982.

be viewed as relatively low. I'll go so far as to say that if money in the bank is 99 percent safe (*nothing* is 100 percent safe!), then money in a money market fund is 96 percent safe.

Another disadvantage of money market funds is that the rate of interest varies almost daily, whereas you get a guaranteed rate of return on your bank deposit. In a rising-interest period, however, your money market fund interest will rise, so the fluctuating interest becomes an advantage then.

There are two ways to reduce the risk involved. The first is by buying only into the largest money funds. The reason for this is that these funds usually carry very prominent names and very substantial backing; given what's at stake, they will do *anything* to protect their fine reputations. Also, and most importantly, the U.S. government has demonstrated that it will not let these large institutions, with billions of American dollars invested in them, fall into jeopardy. There is no doubt in my mind that if one of these multibillion-dollar funds should be in trouble, the government, through the Federal Reserve System, will come to its aid. It is because the smaller funds are less likely to attract government assistance that I recommend you buy only from the largest, best-established funds, thereby letting the government, in an indirect way, be your guarantor. The following list gives the names, addresses, phone numbers, and assets of those money market funds I recommend you stick with.

Dreyfus Liquid Asset Fund
60 Madison Avenue
New York, NY 10022
(800)223-0982
*$11.6 billion in assets**

Fidelity Cash Reserves
Fidelity Daily Income
82 Devonshire Street
Boston, MA 02109
(800)225-6190
$8 billion in assets

Intercapital Liquid Assets
(Contact any branch office
    of Dean Witter)
$9.6 billion in assets

Merrill Lynch Ready Assets
(Contact any branch office
    of Merrill Lynch)
$22.8 billion in assets

Paine Webber Cashfund
(Contact any branch office
of Paine Webber)
$6.7 billion in assets

Cash Reserve Management
(Contact any branch office
of E. F. Hutton)
$7.1 billion in assets

Shearson Daily Dividend
Fund
2 World Trade Center
New York, NY 10048
(Contact any branch of Shear-
son/American Express)
$6.5 billion in assets

Note that the above list of the seven largest money market mutual funds does not necessarily match the list of mutual fund families (groups) on pages 42–43. Only the Dreyfus and Fidelity groups are on both lists and thus are recommended for both purposes.

The majority of the largest money market funds are affiliated with brokerage houses. Although they do have other mutual funds, these others are generally load funds and thus not recommended as a family of funds or for switching purposes.

A more direct way to reduce your risk to almost zero is to buy money market funds that invest only in U.S. government or U.S. agency securities, which is true of the following three funds, which I also recommend.

AARP (American Association
of Retired Persons)
421 Seventh Avenue
Pittsburgh, PA 15219
(800)245-2999
*$4.6 billion in assets**

Capital Preservation Fund
755 Page Mill Road
Palo Alto, CA 94304
(800)472-3389
$2.3 billion in assets

Merrill Lynch Government
Fund
(Contact any branch of Mer-
rill Lynch)
$2.8 billion in assets

---

*Assets as of end of 1982.

The cost of additional safety that these funds offer is usually a 1 percent to 1½ percent reduction in the annual rate of return. Remember, though, that you can indirectly get the government behind you by purchasing your money market shares from the largest funds, and it won't cost you an additional 1 percent to 1½ percent.

Bank Money Market Funds

At the beginning of 1983, the government began allowing banks to issue money market accounts. These accounts are similar to the money market mutual funds as we have described them. The advantage of the bank fund is that it carries an FDIC insurance guarantee. There are, however, two disadvantages. The first disadvantage is that you have no switching privileges, as you do with the mutual fund families. The second disadvantage is that you must go into the bank fund with a minimum of $2,500. Then, if your balance falls below $2,500 once you have opened the account, your rate of return reverts to the 5½ percent passbook rate. Since most of my recommendations in the area of mutual funds suggest initial deposits of less than $2,500, bank money market funds do not really serve our purpose.

You should know, however, that notwithstanding the $2,500 minimum, bank funds offer rates that are, indeed, comparable to large fund accounts (although the banks have, for promotional reasons, offered higher returns, of 11 percent to 13 percent and more, for the first month that the account was opened). If you decide, for one reason or another, to open a bank money market fund, invest with the largest commercial bank for added safety.

But, as I say, unless extenuating circumstances exist, you're best off depositing your money market mutual fund money with a large mutual fund.

Maximum Capital Gains Mutual Funds

Whereas money market funds represent the least risky side of mutual fund investing, maximum capital gains mutual funds are at the opposite end of the spectrum, involving the highest risks within the area of mutual funds. Also known as *performance funds, aggressive growth funds,* and *special situation funds,* these companies try to maximize capital appreciation (long-term profit) of your money with little or no regard for short-term profit (current income). They do this by investing in small, new companies they feel have the best chances of growing over a long period. The prospectuses of these funds state up front that capital gains are their objective and that higher-than-average risks will be taken to achieve their goal. They also tell you that portfolio turnover for these funds usually is higher than average.

These funds are attractive because in the long run they can be expected to do substantially better than the stock market, in which they invest primarily. However, given the risk involved, I do not recommend that they constitute a major portion of any investor's portfolio.

The typical objective of this type of fund would be that of the Twentieth-Century Growth Fund. Their prospectus states:

> . . . primary investment objective is capital growth, growth through a policy retaining maximum flexibility (high turnover rate) in the management of its portfolio. . . . It is management's intention that the portfolio will generally consist of common stocks.[3]

Note that the term "maximum flexibility" refers to the fact that this fund is likely to utilize a high turnover rate of their investments to achieve maximum returns.

The objective of the T. Rowe Price New Horizon Fund,

---

[3]*Weisenberger Investment Company Services,* 1982 edition, page 461.

Table 1.
Increase (or Decrease) in Value of Three High-Performance Mutual Funds (in Percent), 1972–82

	1972	1973	1974	1975	1976
Fidelity Magellan Fund* 82 Devonshire Street Boston, MA 02109 (800)225-6190	30.9	–42.1	–28.3	44.4	37.7
Scudder Development Fund 175 Federal Street Boston, MA 02110 (800)225-2470	31.0	–46.1	–47.1	77.9	22.8
Twentiety-Century Growth Fund P.O. Box 200 Kansas City, MO 64141 (816)531-5575	42.5	–21.5	–30.5	41.7	61.1
Dow-Jones Industrial Average (with all dividends reinvested)	—	—	—	—	—

whose goal is also maximum capital growth, is stated as follows:

> The objective of the fund is long-term growth of capital through investment primarily in small growth companies which management believes have the potential to become major companies in the future.[4]

As you can see, the objectives of these companies are

[4]Ibid., page 391.

50

1977	1978	1979	1980	1981	5 Years (Through 6/30/82)	10 Years (Through 6/30/82)
14.5	31.7	51.7	69.9	16.4	297.8	263.8
25.2	29.9	29.9	46.6	9.0	181.0	83.8
13.8	47.5	74.2	73.3	−5.6	269.7	314.0
—	—	—	—	—	—	−12.6

*In 1983 the Fidelity Magellan Fund purchase fee increased from 2 to 3 percent. Therefore, this fund is recommended only for·buy and hold strategies and not for situations in which switching often is foreseen.

Source: Weisenberger Investment Company Services, 1982 edition.

similar; however, their means of achieving their goals vary.

Table 1 illustrates the performance of three maximum capital gains funds whose objective is to maximize capital appreciation; I recommend these funds to those investors for whom this type of investment was prescribed in Chapter 3. These three funds are recommended for their past performance, their objectives, and their strategies in both bull (rising) and bear (declining) markets.

As you can see from the table, year-to-year performance varies greatly, thus further indicating the risk involved.

But as I've mentioned, with this higher risk comes potentially higher returns. Note that over the past ten years, the value of these funds increased from almost 84 percent to 314 percent,[5] an impressive performance indeed, especially since, as the table shows, the Dow-Jones Industrial Average, representing performance of the stock market, with all dividends reinvested, *declined* 12.6 percent. When you further consider that during that ten-year period the cost of living doubled, you can see just how well two of the three funds shown outpaced inflation.

In dealing with maximum capital gains funds, remember that the potential high rate of return is definitely there, but not without commensurate risk. Do not ignore the performance levels for the years 1973 and 1974, which Table 1 illustrates. You might recall that those were the years when the stock market did particularly poorly; as you can see, these mutual funds accentuated the poor performance.

Notwithstanding these precautions, these funds are excellent for investors who can afford a higher level of risk in order to take advantage of potentially higher returns later.

Growth Stock Mutual Funds

The typical objective of the growth stock mutual fund is long-term capital growth, much the same as for the maximum capital gains funds, but with a secondary eye out for current income. Rather than invest in newer, smaller companies, these funds put their (your) money into the stock of large, established companies that have proved themselves by performing well over time. Thus the risk is less than that for the maximum capital gains mutual funds mentioned previously. The growth stock mutual fund is ideal for the more conservative individual interested in long-term high returns who also wants to keep abreast of

---

[5]Assuming all dividends were reinvested.

inflation—and who doesn't?—but as always, there's the risk to consider.

Again the objectives of this type of fund are clearly stated in the prospectus, as in the case of the Scudder Common Stock Fund:

> . . . long-term growth of capital, and to reach this objective, management invests primarily in selected common stocks. For the most part, management limits its purchase to seasoned and readily marketable securities of leading companies listed in the National Securities Exchange.[6]

Similarly, the objective of the Value Line Fund is stated as follows:

> . . . appreciation of capital and income consistent with a "growth" objective. . . . A flexible investment policy enables management to shift from stocks to bonds. . . .[7]

The Windsor Fund outlines the following objective:

> Long-term growth of capital and income, through investment in equity securities, is the primary objective. However, the fund may invest, without restriction, in high-grade bonds and preferred stocks. Emphasis is on industries and companies believed to have particularly favorable long-term prospects for appreciation, based on increasing earnings and dividends.[8]

Table 2 shows the rates of return for 1972–82 for the three long-term-growth mutual funds I recommend. Note that for that period, Value Line Fund increased 184 percent in value while Scudder Common Stock Fund in-

---

[6]*Weisenberger Investment Companies Services*, 1982 edition, page 417.
[7]*Weisenberger Investment Companies Services*, 1982 edition, page 475.
[8]Ibid., page 477.

	1972	1973	1974	1975	1976
Scudder Common Stock Fund 175 Federal Street Boston, MA 02110 (800)225-2470	18.0	–20.2	–30.7	34.3	25.1
Value Line Fund 711 Third Avenue New York, NY 10007 (800)223-0828	10.5	–29.7	–22.4	39.2	42.5
Windsor Fund (of Vanguard Group) P.O. Box 2600 Valley Forge, PA 19482 (800)524-7025	10.2	–25.0	–16.8	54.5	46.4
Down-Jones Industrial Average (With all dividends reinvested)	—	—	—	—	—

creased 59.1 percent and Windsor went up 161 percent.
Compare these figures to the Dow Jones Industrial Average,
which *decreased* 12.6 percent for the ten-year period, and
you can see that, again, these funds offer a terrific hedge
against both inflation and direct stock market investments.

How to Invest in Mutual Funds

To get started investing in the funds that I have recommended in this chapter, all of which are no-load funds,
write to the addresses given or call the toll-free numbers

1977	1978	1979	1980	1981	5 Years (Through 6/30/82)	10 Years (Through 6/30/82)
−1.6	10.8	23.4	34.4	−6.1	59.7	59.1
9.5	19.3	44.0	41.6	2.4	145.4	184.0
1.0	8.8	22.6	22.9	16.8	31.9	161.0
—	—	—	—	—	—	−12.6

Source: *Weisenberger Investment Company Services,* 1982 edition.

and request the prospectus and application form. Read thoroughly all the material you receive, making sure that the objectives and risks stated are consistent with your own intentions. The material you receive will contain charts showing past performance; review these carefully and compare them to the performance charts of other funds.

Check the prospectus for various services they offer, such as telephone and telex withdrawals and other convenient withdrawal plans. If you're investing in one of the families of funds, find out whether there will be a charge for switching from one fund to another. In the case of money market funds, be sure to request check-writing privileges, which will enable you to use that fund as a high-interest-bearing checking account. If you have questions about the material, call the toll-free number. Be aggressive with your questions. Remember, it's your money—and your future—you are dealing with; you have a right to understand every aspect of your investment. Use what you have learned in this chapter; invest wisely enough and you may not be a small investor forever.

5

IRAs

The Individual Retirement Accounts, commonly called IRAs, are probably the most beneficial, interesting tax shelter for the middle class since the introduction of tax deductibility on mortgage interest payments. That is, IRAs are most definitely an extremely favorable investment alternative that should not be overlooked by *any* tax-fearing citizen.

What is this new tax shelter for the middle class? Why was it instituted? A bit of history answers these questions.

IRA laws were first set up in 1975. At that time, however, they were made available only to employed people whose employers did not cover them under any pension plan. This, indeed, turned out to be a vast minority. Furthermore, the maximum annual contribution was 15 percent of your income or $1,500, whichever was less, which graduated to $1,750 if your spouse also was employed. Under these restrictions, IRAs were not very popular, nor were they available to the people who needed them most.

But with the passage of the Economic Recovery Act of 1981, everything changed for the IRAs. The floodgates were open at last, and IRAs became available to practically all gainfully employed people regardless of whether they had a pension plan. IRAs quickly became the object of great attention, not to mention books, TV programs, and magazine articles. Major banks centered entire ad campaigns on them, and I know few accountants or investment counselors who did not recommend them. I feel just as strongly about them, but the important things for you to understand about these tax shelters are the obvious and hidden advantages they offer as well as the risks involved.

Why did the government institute them? For three basic reasons. In the first place, they felt that the plan would be highly popular among their constituents (remember the voters). In the second place, it became obvious that average citizens were in great need of a plan that would give them pension incomes in addition to Social Security, which, it became obvious, was running into difficulties. (In fact, you will find that the Social Security program will most likely see major changes in the coming decade.) Finally, from an economic point of view, the new IRAs would increase the savings—and eventually the buyer power—of retirees, proving quite helpful for the long-term growth of the economy.

Now for the important part—how IRAs can benefit the 116 million people[1] who are eligible for them.

Under the new laws, you can invest up to 100 percent of your income or a maximum of $2,000 a year, whichever is less, in these IRAs. This $2,000 is tax-deductible, so that if you're earning $25,000 a year and you contribute $2,000 to an IRA, your income, in the eyes of the IRS, is $23,000. Thus, if you are in the 35 percent tax bracket,[2] this $2,000 deduction actually is worth $700 (35 percent of $2,000) which you have kept from the pocket of the IRS and instead put in your own. Not bad, right? But stay with me; it gets better.

---

[1]See *IRAs—Your Complete Money Guide* by the editors of *Money* magazine, 1982.

[2]This is roughly the bracket for single persons with an adjusted gross income of $25,000.

If your spouse does not work, you can invest $2,250 in an IRA on a tax-deductible basis. But if your spouse takes a job, even on a part-time basis, earning as little as $40 a week, then the maximum contribution becomes $4,000 a year. To recap: If you are earning $25,000 a year and your spouse earns an additional $2,000, bringing your joint annual income up to $27,000, you may place $4,000 in an IRA account, and your total tax savings becomes 35 percent of that $4,000, for a grand total of $1,400.

This advantage is fairly easy to recognize, but there is an even more overwhelming advantage, for the law says that you can invest that IRA money in a variety of ways, which I will discuss later. For now, it is important to see that the income you accrue on those investments is tax-deferred until the money is withdrawn, usually at retirement. Thus you're earning interest and dividends on the money you would have paid to the IRS had you not opened an IRA.

Chances are you've heard various claims regarding the fact that if you set up an IRA account now, you can be a millionaire by the time you retire. Yes, it's true, and here are the numbers to prove it. Note that the figures shown indicate what would happen to your money if you invested it at a 12 percent interest rate, which is a reasonable expected return.

Table 1.
IRA Deposits of $2,000 Invested Annually at 12 Percent Interest Rate

Years to Retirement	Amount Deposited	Amount at Withdrawal (at Retirement)	
10	$20,000	$41,500	
15	30,000	91,000	
20	40,000	181,000	
25	50,000	348,000	
30	60,000	654,000	
35	70,000	1,216,000	(You're a millionaire!)

As the table shows, in less than thirty-five years you can accumulate $1 million by investing a mere $2,000 annually into an IRA. The beauty of it is that you are compounding returns that would otherwise have been paid to the IRS. Compare this situation to one in which you were to place $2,000 annually into a 12 percent return taxable investment. At the end of thirty-five years you would have only about $350,000, as opposed to over $1 million in your IRA.

The main reason people hesitate to open an IRA is that they feel that they cannot afford to put all that money away for so many years. They fear they may need the money prior to retirement. True, the law says you may not withdraw the money until age 59½ (and that you *must* start withdrawing the funds by age 70½). This seems quite reasonable, given that most people do indeed retire by the time they reach 65. The key question, then, given that we have already learned the importance of the flexibility of your investments, is: Will the money be available before you reach age 59½? Happily, the answer is a resounding *yes*. The law goes on to say that if you become permanently disabled, you may withdraw your funds, and in this case, no early-withdrawal penalty will be due, except, of course, for the taxes that will be owed normally.

Another favorable aspect of your IRA is that at your death, at whatever age, your designated beneficiary may receive up to $100,000 of the money in your account *tax free*. That's right; by setting up an IRA, you are actually planning a tax-free estate of up to $100,000. Remember: You didn't pay taxes on this money originally, you haven't paid taxes on the annual income accrued, and now your beneficiary receives it tax-free as well.[3] That's hard to beat, no matter what investment game you're playing.

But what if you'd simply like to have the money earlier for emergencies or for personal or financial reasons? Will the money be there for you then? Again, the answer is yes, and it is for this reason that I advocate IRAs without hesitation. The problem here (yes, there's a catch) is that

---

[3]Instituted under the Tax Equity and Fiscal Responsibility Act of 1982.

you will be charged a 10 percent penalty on funds withdrawn prematurely. But this is hardly a drawback when you consider that the law could easily have barred *any* early withdrawals. Furthermore, as I will show you in a moment, in the case where you have decided to withdraw the money, after a sufficient period of time *you would be no worse off than if you had never opened the IRA in the first place*.

A word of warning is in order here, though: I do not advise you to open an IRA if you *know* that you're going to want to get your hands on those funds soon. Set up an IRA with the full intention of using it for your retirement. Let's face it: You'll need it then. But with the economy and world situation changing now as rapidly as it has been, it's certainly nice to have your options open.

What happens if you find that you need your money sooner than at retirement? The answer can be had by following a $2,000 investment both with and without an IRA plan. For the sake of simplicity, let's suppose that the following individual making these investments is in the 50 percent tax bracket. Here's what happens to a $2,000 IRA investment to be withdrawn after six years.

Initial IRA investment	$2,000
Value in six years at 12 percent annual rate of return	4,000
Less 50 percent taxes	−2,000
	$2,000
Less 10 percent early-withdrawal penalty	−400
Net worth after taxes and penalty	$1,600

This individual is left with $1,600. But suppose this person did not invest in an IRA but instead invested in a

12 percent non-IRA account, again being in the 50 percent tax bracket.

Initial investment	$2,000
Less 50 percent taxes	−1,000
	$1,000
Net worth in six years at 12 percent annual rate of return*	$1,420

As you can see, that IRA investment, with penalty and taxes included, still is worth more than the non-IRA investment. The point is that even if you must withdraw your money from an IRA account early, you are no worse off than you would be if you had never opened the account. In short, you have nothing to lose.[4]

Reviewing the information discussed thus far, you can shelter $2,000 a year and tax-defer all income on it until retirement. You can set up this plan even if you are currently covered under a pension plan. Early withdrawals are permitted, but with a 10 percent penalty and all taxes due, as with ordinary income, which should be viewed as tolerable if the money is really needed.

The Various Types of IRA Accounts

The next critical question is: Which investments do the IRA laws honor, or what can you invest in and still be eligible for IRA benefits? The law here is quite liberal; you can invest in just about anything except for life insurance

---

*Although the rate of return is 12 percent every year, 50 percent taxes must be paid, so the annual after-tax return is actually 6 percent, which this total takes into account.

[4]Note that you *would* be worse off if you decided to withdraw the money after two years instead of six. For this reason, as I say, open the account with every intention of leaving the money there until retirement.

policies, precious metals (silver, gold, etc.), and collectibles. By collectibles they mean works of art, rugs or antiques, metals or gems, stamps or coins, alcoholic beverages, or any other tangible personal property as specified by the IRS.[5] So those Rembrandts and Picassos are out, along with rubies and Chippendale furniture. What's left? Actually, a very respectable assortment of investments from which to choose, including stocks, bonds, mutual funds, annuities, treasury notes, and similar vehicles. Remember that the government set up the new IRA plans for its own purposes as well as yours. Investing in these items, rather than the ones that are barred from IRA rulings, will benefit the economy in one way or another. Clever fellows, aren't they?

Before you begin to consider the IRA investment opportunities open to you, it is important that you stop and think about your own financial objectives. Can you accept the concept of risk both financially and psychologically? To what extent? Is it important for you to know that your money is fully guaranteed at all times, or are you willing to assume some additional risk to gain a potentially higher return? The answers to these questions will help you to choose among the alternatives presented below.

The following self-analysis table presents some ideas concerning safety and risk and then indicates which IRA investment vehicles are your best bet based on the information your responses reveal. Take a few moments to answer the questions as realistically as you can. To take the test, after each of the statements circle the number that comes closest to describing your preference. If the statement is very important to you, circle 5; if it hardly matters to you, circle 1, and so on. The column at the right shows which IRA investment vehicles best meet your priorities.

---

[5]*The 1981 Economic Recovery Tax Act*, Research Institute of America, New York, 1981.

Table 2.
Which IRA Plan Is Best for You?

How Important Is This?	Very Important			Not Important		Your Best Bet
1. Federally assisted assets	5	4	3	2	1	Banks
2. Fixed interest rates	5	4	3	2	1	Banks
3. The chance to earn big profits quickly	5	4	3	2	1	Mutual funds
4. Access to your money before retirement at the lowest penalty	5	4	3	2	1	Mutual funds
5. No obstacles to contributing less than $2,000 a year	5	4	3	2	1	Banks, mutual funds
6. Easy switching among stocks, bonds, and money market funds	5	4	3	2	1	Mutual fund families
7. An account with no charges	5	4	3	2	1	Many banks, many mutual funds
8. An investment yield that changes with other interest rates	5	4	3	2	1	Banks, mutual funds
9. Very high rate of return with no risk whatsoever	5	4	3	2	1	Not available anywhere

Your circled answers will tell you a lot concerning how you feel about financial risk. For instance, if you circled 5 for statements 1 and 2 and you circled 1 for statement 3, your strong preference is for safety—insured principal with a fixed rate of return. As the table shows, a bank probably is the best place for you to satisfy your investment objectives. Your response to statement 3 further confirms that high-risk investments simply are not your cup of tea.

Your response to statement 5 was most likely a 5; note, however, that this feature simply is not available anywhere, the point being: Be realistic in your demands!

Although there are numerous investment vehicles open to the IRA investor, I feel strongly that the two best options for the inexperienced small investor are banks and mutual funds. Thus I will be limiting my discussion to these two groups.

Your IRA Bank Account

For the investor in search of a very safe, convenient vehicle involving no fee whatsoever, banks—the largest commercial ones, that is—can't be beat. Your funds will be insured up to $100,000 by the government via the FDIC. Of course, in less than twenty years your IRA probably will be worth more than $100,000, at which point you may want to divide your funds between two banks. But by that time FDIC insurance may cover funds up to $300,000.

Banks offer basically two types of IRA accounts: the *fixed-interest account;* and the *variable-rate account,* in which your interest rate changes with market interest rate fluctuations.

Fixed-rate certificates vary as to the length of time during which the interest rate is guaranteed. Some start at eighteen months and go up to thirty months and even four years; some banks, although not many, will even guarantee a rate for as long as ten years.

Like shopping for anything else, you'll want to look around for the best possible situation for your IRA money. Why? Well, for one thing, interest rates vary a great deal from bank to bank. In fact, in June 1982, in a study of the 225 largest American banks, it was found that the interest rates on otherwise similar fixed-rate accounts varied by as much as 5 percent; the highest rate reported was over 15½ percent, while the lowest was 11 percent.[6] This point should illustrate the absolute necessity for shopping around before you decide which bank to do business with.

Another thing to look for when shopping around for a bank is the rate at which your interest will be compounded, called the *effective annual yield*. Each time your interest is computed, the principal taken into account consists of the amount you invested *plus* the amount of that previous interest payment. The best situation, therefore, is the one in which the interest is computed most often. As you review the advantages of various banks, you'll find that some pay interest daily while others compute it quarterly, semi-annually, and so on. Bear in mind that the difference between a 14 percent yield compounded annually and a 14 percent yield compounded daily could amount to tens of thousands of dollars by the time you draw out your IRA funds at retirement. For this reason, do not open an IRA account with any bank without knowing what the effective annual yield is, for without it, comparisons become extremely difficult.

Once you have chosen a bank with whom you would like to do business, you will next have to choose between a fixed-interest account and a variable-rate account. The former guarantees that a given interest rate will be paid for the duration of the account. If you believe that interest rates probably will go down during the time period involved, or if you just don't know, then the fixed-interest account is for you. The safety measure you ensure here, of course, is that if interest rates do drop, you still go on receiving the rate that prevailed at the time you purchased your certificate. Of course, this is a two-way street: If interest rates go up, you're stuck with the one you signed up for. Thus the price of safety.

If you believe that interest rates will rise and you're

---

[6]The study was conducted by Brent L. Rufener and published in the *IRA/Keogh Guide*, P.O. Box 32, Midvale, UT 84047.

prepared to put your money where your beliefs are, you'll want to go with the variable-rate account. The interest rates on these accounts change weekly. The changes are based on a predetermined market interest rate; commonly used benchmarks are the annualized yields on thirteen-week, twenty-six-week, or one-year treasury bills. These variable-rate accounts, by the way, last for eighteen months. The beauty of these, of course, is that if interest rates rise, so do your returns. But again, it works both ways: You could find yourself at the mercy of declining rates as well.

The choice, then, between fixed- and variable-rate accounts should be fairly simple, except for one thing: The government currently has a ceiling on how high interest rates can go. These ceilings, however, will expire by 1986, and so the government has devised a special eighteen-month "wild card" account exempting bank IRAs from normal interest-rate ceilings. The rates on these accounts vary widely, so again, comparison shopping becomes important.

To recap what we've discussed about bank IRAs: For maximum safety, convenience, reasonable rates of return, personal attention, and no-fee investments, banks are your best bet. You will have to decide between 18-month variable-rate accounts and the 18- to 120-month fixed-rate accounts. Happy dart-throwing!

To open the IRA account you've chosen, you need only explain your intention to a bank clerk. You will be given the proper forms to be filled out, and the bank then will notify the IRS of the account. Indicate, when you open the account, that you would like to be notified when the account reaches maturity so you will have the option of renewing it or changing it to another type. Otherwise the bank is likely to renew it automatically.

If you decide at the end of the time period to switch to another account, another bank, or another type of institution altogether, such as a mutual fund, simply notify the new institution and let it handle the paperwork. The transaction will take place automatically. Of course, as long as you are switching to another IRA account, no taxes will be due.

As with any other investment, feel free to ask questions, and be sure to insist on clear, understandable answers. Compare rates and other circumstances, for these change from bank to bank. These days, some banks offer premiums (toasters, luggage, etc.) for your new IRA account. Stay away from these promotions; one way or another you do, of course, pay for those goodies.

Your Mutual Fund IRA

If the personal analysis chart you filled out on page 64 indicated that you were willing and able to take certain risks to reap greater potential returns, you will want to pursue your IRA interests through mutual funds. Chapter 4 explains mutual funds in detail, so read that chapter now if you haven't already done so. Briefly, as Chapter 4 explains, the funds I recommend are all no-load, or noncommission funds offered by the largest mutual fund families.

Although there are many different types of mutual funds from which to choose, I recommend only two of them for your IRA investment: the relatively safe, highly liquid money market funds, and the high-risk maximum capital gains funds. The former of these invests in short-term obligations of the U.S. government, major corporations, and large commercial banks. The accounts are highly liquid, quite safe (although not guaranteed by the FDIC), and offer reasonable rates of return. Maximum capital gains funds, on the other hand, are high-risk, potentially high-performance funds that emphasize maximum rates of return with little emphasis on short-term performance. Their goal is to maximize long-term appreciation of capital, and they fulfill these pursuits largely by purchasing common stocks of smaller, newer companies and by employing other speculative investment techniques.[7] These funds are quite risky, with rates of return going up as much as 25 to 50 percent in some years and down a similar amount during other years. However, over the past five years[8] some of these funds have had a total return of 200 to 300 percent.

The question, as far as your IRA money is concerned, is not necessarily which of these two highly divergent funds to choose, but *how to divide your money between them to obtain a proper portfolio mix*. The reason for splitting them at all has to do with offsetting the risk involved, much as the mutual funds hedge their bets by investing in a large variety of places. Thus a loss at one end is minimized by a hopefully more successful return at the other end.

Again, you will have to ask yourself some questions about how much risk you are willing to take, and again, if the answer is none at all, then go back to your first choice, banks. But if you are willing to take some risk in the hope of obtaining a higher return, read on.

Table 3 will help you decide exactly what your IRA portfolio mix should be.

Table 3.
Your IRA Portfolio Mix

Type of Investor	Percentage of IRA Investment in Money Market Fund	Percentage of IRA Investment in Maximum Capital Gains Fund
Very low risk	100	0
Low risk	85–95	5–15
Moderate risk	70–85	15–30
High risk	40–70	30–60

[7]A complete discussion of how these funds work and how you can set up your account can be found in Chapter 4.

[8]For the five-year period ending June 30, 1982.

Look at the column on the left and decide which type of investor most closely resembles your own priorities. As you can see, the low-risk investor (not to be confused with the no-risk investor) should have a portfolio consisting of approximately 90 percent money market fund investments and 10 percent maximum capital gains investments. At the other end of the extreme, the high-risk investor may have as much as 50 percent of his or her money in each type of fund. I would not recommend that anyone place 100% of their IRA money into a maximum capital gains mutual fund, since the risk inherent in this type of fund simply is not acceptable for needed retirement income. Although these aggressive funds have done quite well during the past five years, the risk definitely is there, and we can rarely count on history repeating itself.

Once you've determined the portfolio mix best for you, refer to Chapter 4 for instructions on opening these accounts.

The questions we posed at the beginning of this chapter did not ask whether or not an IRA should be opened, but how to set one up and choose from the myriad of choices available. I recommend these accounts wholeheartedly to almost all types of investors for the simple reason that IRAs are one of the great options open to us today that enable us to grab a bit of financial security to be enjoyed later. I urge you to recognize this opportunity for what it is, to explore its various features, and to take advantage of the rewards it offers.

6

Government Securities

Every week of the year the United States government borrows money. The IOU's they exchange for the money they have borrowed are known as government securities, which are generally referred to as *bonds*.[1]

All bonds have some basic things in common. For one thing, the interest received on U.S. government bonds always is exempt from state and local taxes, and this is a key feature of their attractiveness to investors.

In terms of how they work, all government securities have some other things in common as well. First of all, they all have a maturity date; that is the date at which the bondholders receive back their original principal. Here's how it works: When you buy a bond, the value of that bond, despite what you pay for it, is $1,000, or something very close to it.[2] This is referred to as the *par value* of the bond. At the maturity date the bondholder receives back its par value, or $1,000 per bond.

---

[1]Not to be confused with *savings bonds*, which are quite different and which will be explained later in this chapter. The points made in the discussion at hand exclude savings bonds in many respects.

[2]Day-to-day changes in interest rates result in minor price adjustments.

The second thing all bonds have in common is a *coupon rate;* that is the initial rate of return, or yield, which is determined by current interest rates at the time the bond is purchased. For example, suppose you buy a ten-year bond in 1982 that will mature in 1992. The par value is $1,000, and the going interest rate, when you buy this bond, is 11 percent. That means you get $110 a year ($1,000 multiplied by 11 percent) for each of the ten years you hold the bond. Here you can see two constants at work: (1) the par value, which never changes; and (2) a coupon rate—a set amount that will be paid each year no matter what, until maturity.

There is one variable, and it comes into play if you decide to sell the bond before it matures, which is quite common. The variable is the price at which you would sell that $1,000 bond. You purchased it in 1982 at an 11 percent coupon rate. Let's say that in 1983 you decide to sell it. By that time, we'll suppose, interest rates have gone up to 13 percent, so that newly issued ten-year bonds maturing in 1993 are paying $130 a year, not the $110 you are receiving. Who will buy your bond paying $110 a year when they could be getting $130? Nobody, except maybe your mother. So how can you sell it? By selling it at a discount that will enable a buyer to make up the annual return that he or she would be missing out on by purchasing your older bond. In this instance you would call your broker or the bank from which you purchased the bond to find out its *current market value.* The price you are quoted will depend almost totally on the current level of interest rates. In the case of the imaginary bond under discussion, the market value probably would be about $900, as opposed to the $1,000 you paid.[3]

The lesson inherent in this illustration is crucial to un-

---

[3]The mathematics involved in arriving at the current market value of the bond are fairly complicated and beyond the level of this discussion. Depend on your broker or bank, then, to give you the proper selling price.

derstanding how bonds work: *As interest rates go up, the market price of existing bonds goes down*. And the longer the maturity of the bond, the greater the risk that interest rates will rise, devaluating the market price of your bond in the process. This brings us to my prime rule of thumb about government securities: *Do not buy long-term bonds*. The risk that your initial investment will be jeopardized is far too great, even for a U.S. government money instrument.

The answer to the problem lies in purchasing short-term bonds with maturities of one year or less. The risk is far less, since shorter-term securities are *not* so sensitive to interest-rate changes. Thus it is unlikely that you will lose out due to changing rates.

Short-term bonds carrying maturity dates of one year or less are called *treasury bills* and are considered to be low-risk investments. Those bonds with maturities from two to seven years, issued by the U.S. government, are called *treasury notes*. These, as you probably can guess, carry a greater amount of risk than treasury bills, but they carry less risk than the long-term *treasury bonds,* which are securities that have maturity dates over seven years. These are different from the commonly known savings bonds. Treasury notes generally pay higher interest rates. Actually, under certain conditions, I do recommend them, but only those that have maturities of five years or less.

Why the Government Issues Securities

The United States owes over $1 trillion. To appreciate the size of that number better, consider that one trillion is equal to one thousand billion, or, as it is written, 1,000,000,000,000.

With a debt of over $1 trillion (and you thought you had problems!), as you can imagine, the government always is looking for ways to borrow money. In addition to the current debt, they must constantly pay off treasury bills, treasury notes, and treasury bonds that mature each week of the year. These additional headaches result in the government accruing over $200 billion in new debts annually. And if the government has to raise even more money each year to cope with a budget *deficit* (the difference between the amount of money they owe and the amount they have on hand), as is currently the case, they must issue even more securities. As you can see, the beat goes on.

The original theory behind government debt supposed that in times of poor economy or war, the government would borrow funds to fill their present needs. When the economy improved and/or peace ensued, the deficits would become a surplus of funds, and the debts would be paid off slowly. That sounded pretty good in theory, but the truth is, unfortunately, that the last year when the U.S. government budget was in surplus was in 1958, under President Eisenhower (remember Ike?).

For fiscal year 1983 the federal *deficit* is estimated to be over $150 billion, and a "conservative" White House estimate predicts that in 1984 it will approach $200 billion. This staggering need for funds by the government, then, remains a constant benefit to the wise investor. Additionally, it exerts an upward pressure on interest rates.

The Various Types of Marketable Government Securities

The government issues many different types of securities. Marketable securities, meaning those that are negotiable, or transferrable, as opposed to savings bonds, which are not, fall into three main categories: treasury bills, treasury notes, and treasury bonds. The reason for issuing three different types of securities is basically a marketing strategy: The variety attracts different types of investors. We can now examine each different category—and their buyers—more closely.

I have often been asked, What is the safest investment in the world today? Without reservation, my answer always is U.S. treasury bills—for a number of reasons. They are short-term investments, of one year or less. As we've seen, this is of the utmost importance in an active money market, such as the one we are presently experiencing. Treasury bills also are very liquid: They can be resold easily. And they involve a small chance of loss; if held to maturity, their par value is guaranteed. Sold before maturity in an active money market, a neat rate of return still is possible.

The final reason that I call these the safest investment around today is that they represent a direct obligation of the U.S. government and as such are sold not only domestically, but internationally as well. The ultimate guarantee here is that if the government were not able to pay off these treasury bills (or any securities, for that matter) at maturity (in which case worse would have come to the very worst), they could literally print the money they needed to do so.[4] For these reasons, then, I view treasury bills as the safest money instruments to be had anywhere and recommend them often to my clients.

Each Monday at 1:30 P.M. the government issues over $10 billion in three- and six-month treasury bills, or T-bills, as they are affectionately known. The amount issued may vary from time to time, but they always are sold on Mondays at 1:30 P.M. The one-year treasury bills are sold every four weeks. (The nine-month treasury bills of yesteryear are no longer issued.)

We've already noted the advantages of treasury bills. Their disadvantage is that they must be bought ten at a time—that is, ten T-bills for $10,000. When they were

---

[4]The consequences of this highly questionable practice are beyond the scope of this book but are explained fully in any comprehensive text on the history of inflation. Moreover, while the government does indeed have the power to issue this new money, in the event that push came to shove, it would be more likely to come up with the money by selling new treasury bills to the Federal Reserve.

first issued, they could be purchased singly, but back in 1970, when interest rates were relatively high, many people made it a common practice to withdraw their money from savings accounts to purchase them. Hundreds of people lined up in downtown Manhattan to make their purchases directly from the Federal Reserve bank. The effect on bank savings was, of course, highly detrimental, and so the government was moved to make ten T-bills the minimum purchase.

Treasury bills are sold a bit differently from most other government securities. They are sold on a *discount basis*. Here's how this works: You can purchase ten T-bills worth $10,000 at an 11 percent interest rate (assuming that is the prevailing rate). But instead of paying $10,000 for them, you pay only $8,900; your 11 percent interest rate is actually deducted from the purchase price. Of course, you receive full par value, $10,000, when your T-bills mature. The difference between the par value and the price you paid is your profit, and it is referred to as the *discount value*.

The great advantage of this system is that you have received your interest in advance. And since you are getting 11 percent on $10,000 while having put up only $8,900, your real rate of return winds up being something closer to 12 percent.

Treasury bills are sold at auction. This does not mean that you have to bid for them. It means that supply and demand—in the form of substantial bidders spending over $250,000 at a clip—determines what becomes an average price, and this is the price that you, the small-bidder with less than $250,000 to spend, will pay. When you buy a T-bill, then, you won't actually know exactly what your discount will be until after the auction has taken place.

There are two basic ways to purchase T-bills. You can buy them directly from a Federal Reserve bank, or you can get them through a commercial bank or broker.

To purchase T-bills through the Federal Reserve bank nearest you (consult the list on pages 78–81), simply phone for the necessary information and application forms.

The advantage to this method of purchase is that no fee is involved. Also, the Federal Reserve bank will, if you desire, automatically purchase additional T-bills for you when your present ones mature. The disadvantage here is that purchasing through the Federal Reserve bank requires you to produce the par value up front. (Within a few weeks they refund the difference between the par value and the price you actually have to pay.) Upon making your purchase, you will receive a statement showing the number of bills you have purchased and their maturity date.

Purchasing T-bills through a commercial bank or broker with whom you have an account is somewhat simpler. Assuming you have enough money in your account to cover the purchase, you simply tell them to put in a buy order for the number of bills you would like to purchase. This order will be put through for the following Monday when the T-bills are issued. The bank or broker will charge your account when the proceeds are needed, usually the following Thursday. If there is a chance that you will be selling your T-bills before they reach maturity, having purchased them from a commercial bank or broker may make the transaction easier, since you can only buy bonds from a Federal Reserve bank; they will not sell them for you. If you have bought them from a Federal Reserve bank and then wish to sell them before maturity, you must first request that the account be transferred to a commercial bank or broker, who will then sell them for you. As you can see, it may be simpler just to maintain an account with a bank or broker who will service all transactions.

The main—and, I think, the only—disadvantage to buying T-bills from banks and brokers is that there usually is a fee for the transaction (usually $25 to $50), but the advantages, in my opinion, outweigh this relatively small fee, with one exception: If you planned on purchasing additional T-bills each time your current holding matured, then buying directly from the Federal Reserve would be the best way.

Otherwise, a commercial bank is worth the additional $25 to $50 cost.

Federal Reserve Banks and Branches

Federal Reserve Bank of Atlanta
104 Marietta Street NW
Atlanta, GA 30303
(404)586-8500

Federal Reserve Bank of Chicago
230 South La Salle Street
Chicago, IL 60904
(312)322-5322

Federal Reserve Bank of Cleveland—Cincinnati Branch
150 East 4th Street
Cincinnati, OH 45202
(513)721-4787

Federal Reserve Bank of Cleveland—Pittsburgh Branch
717 Grant Street
Pittsburgh, PA 15230
(412)261-7800

Federal Reserve Bank of Dallas
400 South Akard
Dallas, TX 75222
(214)651-6111

Federal Reserve Bank of Dallas—El Paso Branch
P.O. Box 100
El Paso, TX 79999
(915)544-4730

Federal Reserve Bank of Dallas—Houston Branch
1701 San Jacinto Street
Houston, TX 77001
mailing: P.O. Box 2578
Houston, TX 77252
(713)659-4433

Federal Reserve Bank of Dallas—San Antonio Branch
126 East Nueva Street
San Antonio, TX 78204
(512)224-2141

Federal Reserve Bank of Minneapolis
250 Marquette Street
Minneapolis, MN 55480
(612)340-2345

Federal Reserve Bank of Minneapolis—Helena Branch
400 North Park Avenue
Helena, MT 59601
(406)442-3860

Federal Reserve Bank of New York
33 Liberty Street
New York, NY 10005
(212)791-5000

Federal Reserve Bank of New York—Buffalo Branch
160 Delaware Street
Buffalo, NY 14202
mailing: P.O. Box 961
Buffalo, NY 14240
(716)849-5000

Federal Reserve Bank of Philadelphia
100 North Sixth Street
Philadelphia, PA 19101
(215)574-6000

Federal Reserve Bank of Richmond
701 East Byrd Street
Richmond, VA 23219
(804)643-1250

Federal Reserve Bank of St. Louis—Louisville Branch
P.O. Box 32710
Louisville, KY 40232
(502)587-7351

Federal Reserve Bank of San Francisco
101 Market Street
San Francisco, CA 94105
mailing: P.O. Box 7702
San Francisco, CA 94120
(415)974-2000

Federal Reserve Bank of San Francisco—Los Angeles
Branch
409 West Olympic Boulevard
Los Angeles, CA 90015
mailing: P.O. Box 2077
Terminal Annex
Los Angeles, CA 90015
(213)683-8323

Federal Reserve Bank of San Francisco—Portland Branch
915 SW Stark Street
Portland, OR 97205
(503)221-5900

Federal Reserve Bank of San Francisco—Salt Lake City
Branch
120 South State Street
Salt Lake City, UT 84111
mailing: P.O. Box 30780
Salt Lake City, UT 84130
(801)322-7900

Federal Reserve Bank of San Francisco—Seattle Branch
1015 Second Avenue
Seattle, WA 98104
mailing: P.O. Box 3567
Terminal Annex
Seattle, WA 98124
(206)442-1376

Treasury Notes

Treasury notes are a liquid, marketable, and reasonably good-yielding investment. They are debt obligations of the U.S. government with maturities of from two to seven years. They differ from treasury bills in a number of respects. First, their usual minimum purchase is only five or $5,000 worth, as opposed to the ten that must be purchased in the case of T-bills. Second, they are not sold on a discount basis; you pay the par value at the time of purchase, and they pay you interest twice a year, at which time checks are sent to you. Buying securities in this manner is known as *buying at face value*, as opposed to *buying at discount*. You get a lovely certificate when you purchase a treasury note that serves as a constant reminder of where your money is.

The most popular treasury note is the two-year note, which as of this writing is sold once a month. Like treasury bills, they are sold through an auction process.

Over the past few years the yield on two-year treasury notes has ranged from 9 to 16 percent. The risk involved in buying them is slightly higher than that with treasury bills, since their maturity is somewhat longer, but two years still is a relatively short time for this sort of investment, and the risk here should not be viewed as substantial. Many investors find that the higher yield serves as a fair compromise between T-bills and these longer-term notes, especially since their minimum purchase requires an outlay of only $5,000.[5]

To find out exactly when treasury bills are being sold, contact your broker, a bank, or the Federal Reserve. Certain newspapers, such as *The Wall Street Journal* and *The New York Times*, announce this information several days ahead of time.

The government also issues three-, four-, and five-year notes, but not as frequently as the two-year notes. These longer-term notes usually are issued every two months, but as the government's needs mount, they may be issued more often than that.

The disadvantage of the longer-term notes is that your risk increases with the longer maturity, since interest rates become harder to predict and since, in these turbulent times, they are most likely to be quite volatile. For this reason, I do not recommend purchasing securities with maturities of longer than five years unless there are extenuating circumstances. These would exist, for instance, in the case of a retired person who is most interested in having a certain guaranteed income over a ten-year period and would not be interested in selling such a bond before maturity.

Once you have found out when treasury notes will be issued, it is quite simple to purchase them, and it is best to do so from the Federal Reserve. (You may purchase them through a broker as well, but since it is so simple to buy them through the Federal Reserve, you might as well do so and avoid the fee that a broker would charge.) Write a letter to the Federal Reserve Bank nearest you (see pages 78–81), using the following form:

---

[5]For treasury notes whose maturation is longer than two years (which we do not recommend here), the minimum purchase usually is $1,000.

Dear Sir:

I am enclosing a check for $5,000 to purchase $5,000 of new, two-year treasury notes to be issued on June 1, 1983 and maturing on June 1, 1985.

The notes should be issued in my name, Henry Jones. My address is _____. My Social Security number is _____. Please send the notes to the above address.

Sincerely,

It is possible, though unnecessary and probably inconvenient, to pick up your treasury notes personally from the bank. Bear in mind that the Federal Reserve fully insures your treasury note purchase and is responsible for mailing it. Thus I recommend having the notes sent to you.

From then on, every six months until maturity, you will receive a U.S. government check (it looks like a tax-refund check) for the amount of interest owed you. When your note matures, you can take the certificate to your bank or a Federal Reserve bank and pick up the par value of the note. There is no fee involved.

Treasury Bonds

The last type of U.S. government marketable IOU is the treasury bond. These have maturities of over seven years and usually are issued for ten-, twenty-, or thirty-year periods. These bonds, as implied earlier in this chapter, definitely are *not* recommended to the small investor (or any private investor as far as I'm concerned) due to their excessive volatility and the market risk involved, but I'll discuss them briefly here to complete the discussion of government securities and for your edification.

These days, long-term government bonds are issued fairly infrequently—about four times a year. When issued, these bonds generally are sold for their par value, $1,000 each, and the minimum purchase is just one. They can be purchased in the same manner as treasury notes. They are

Table 1.
Comparison of Marketable U.S. Government Securities

	Maturity	How Often Sold	Minimum Purchase	Method Sold	Where to Purchase
3-month treasury bills	3 months	once a week	10	discount	commercial bank, broker, Federal Reserve bank
6-month treasury bills	6 months	once a week	10	discount	commercial bank, broker, Federal Reserve bank
1-year treasury bills	1 year	every 4 weeks	10	discount	commercial bank, broker, Federal Reserve bank
2-year treasury notes	2 years	once a month	5	face value	commercial bank, broker, Federal Reserve bank
3- to 7-year treasury notes	3 to 7 years	approximately every 2 months	1	face value	commercial bank, broker, Federal Reserve bank
treasury bonds	over 7 years	4 times a year	1	face value	commercial bank, broker, Federal Reserve bank

sold at face value through the Federal Reserve and their interest rates are established by auction.

The advantage of treasury bonds is that you are guaranteed a given rate of return for a long period of time, although you can, of course, sell them before maturity. But therein lies the chief disadvantage, for you are locked into a fixed rate of return at a time when interest rates are likely to be quite volatile, perhaps causing the market value of your bonds to drop due to an increase in the interest rate.

You might wonder, then, why they are issued at all, since they obviously do not meet the needs of the average investor. But for large institutions, such as pension funds and insurance companies, they surely do serve a purpose. Furthermore, they also serve the interests of speculators rather well. The practices of these types of investors, and a discussion of how they employ the features of treasury bonds, are examined in Chapter 11, "For High Rollers Only."

For the time being, the subject of treasury bonds may be safely dropped.

U.S. Savings Bonds

As I've mentioned earlier, one of the differences between savings bonds and marketable government securities is that savings bonds are not negotiable: They are issued in the name of a specific person and cannot be transferred from one individual to another. Like other government securities, the interest accrued on savings bonds is exempt from state and local taxes. There are, of course, other important and major differences, and these will come to light as I examine savings bonds further.

Most people are familiar with savings bonds. In fact, the only reason I raise the subject here is that you probably have had, or are likely to have, some experience with them. I have not recommended them to any of the groups of investors described in Chapter 3.

In the past, you could buy a savings bond for $37.50 that would be worth $50 at maturity. People often gave them as gifts for weddings, bar mitzvahs, or confirmations; you could buy a $50 gift for just $37.50 and look like a big spender. But savings bonds have changed over the years (what hasn't?), and these changes will interest you if you currently hold any. In fact, if you have series E bonds somewhere in your safe deposit box (check, since these are easily forgotten), be aware that they are scheduled to stop accumulating interest according to the following schedule. If you do not cash them in or convert them to other, newer bonds, which are described below, within the time shown, you will, of course, still be entitled to the face value of the bond, but you will no longer earn additional interest on it.

Table 2.
Series E Extended Maturities

Date of Issue	Date of Maturity	Term of Bond
May 1941–Apr. 1952	May 1981–Apr. 1992	40 years
May 1952–Jan. 1957	Jan. 1992–Sept. 1996	39 years, 8 months
Feb. 1957–May 1959	Jan. 1996–Apr. 1998	38 years, 11 months
June 1959–Nov. 1965	Mar. 1997–Aug. 2003	37 years, 11 months
Dec. 1965–May 1969	Dec. 1992–May 1996	27 years
June 1969–Nov. 1973	Apr. 1995–Sept. 1999	25 years, 10 months
Dec. 1973–June 1980	Dec. 1998–June 2005	25 years

To compete with today's money market type funds, the government, on November 1, 1982, began issuing new series EE savings bonds, which mature in ten years and which pay market interest rates if held longer than five years. The minimum denomination is a $100 bond, which may be purchased for $50.

Although the way in which the return on these new bonds is calculated is somewhat complicated, they still retain many of the same features that originally made U.S. savings bonds the most widely held security in history. They are backed by the full faith and credit of the government and will be replaced if lost, stolen, or destroyed. They can be redeemed at any time after six months from the issue date, although not at the maximum level of interest. They require an initial investment of only $50. As such, they are often included in payroll deduction plans of various employers.

The new series EE bonds, like the old series E bonds, are sold at discount. The interest that accrues is added to the face value when you cash in your bond at maturity. Thus you would get $100 in 1992 for the bond you paid $50 for in 1982.

But unlike the former fixed rate on savings bonds, the new series EE bonds allow savers to keep pace with market changes. Here's how this works: Every six months the rate on the bonds is pegged at 85 percent of the average market rate on five-year treasury notes. At the end of five years the ten semiannual averages are added and compounded to determine the yield on the first five years of the bond. Bonds held for longer than five years accrue additional interest semiannually. The interest you earn is paid to you at maturity or when you sell the bond.

In essence, what happens is that if you hold the bond for more than five years, the government pays you 85 percent of the interest you'd have received had you purchased a five-year treasury note instead. What's more, the interest is *compounded* semiannually.

Although you can't know in advance what the earnings on the bond will be, savers are guaranteed a minimum return of 7½ percent a year on bonds held for longer than five years. Those who hold their bonds for less than five years but more than six months (you're not allowed to redeem them for the first six months) are guaranteed a return of 7½ percent—again, compounded semiannually.

Every six months, in May and November, the Treasury announces the semiannual yield on these bonds. For the six-month period ending April 30, 1983, the applied interest rate was a very respectable 11.09 percent.

Savings bonds may be purchased from and handled by most banks and U.S. financial institutions as well as by federal reserve banks. They are also handled as payroll deductions. There is never any fee involved.

The main disadvantage of these particular savings bonds is that they are completely liquid for the first six months after they are issued. Also, if they are not held for at least five years, their yield is somewhat wanting.

An advantage often overlooked concerning savings bonds is that the federal taxes (as noted, they are exempt from state and local taxes) due on the interest they accrue is deferred until the bond is cashed in. Thus, if you pay $5,000 for $10,000 worth of savings bonds, the tax due on your $5,000 profit is taxable only when your bonds mature. Matters are improved even more when we consider the beauty of the new series HH bonds.

Series EE or series E savings bonds may be exchanged for series HH bonds, and this constitutes a *tax-deferred* conversion. Thus, using our example, you can put the $10,000 worth of matured EE or E bonds into series HH bonds and even further defer the taxes to a later date, at which time, if you wait long enough, you will be taxed at a lower rate upon retirement.

Of course, you can buy series HH bonds without ever having purchased series EE or series E bonds. They are sold in $500 denominations and pay an interest rate of 8½ percent annually, which is computed and compounded semiannually. The interest is then sent directly to you. They carry ten-year maturities.

Again, savings bonds have not been recommended as an investment vehicle simply because higher interest rates and more liquid investments are available on the market today.

Our discussion of government securities illustrates the interesting fact that because of its insatiable need to finance its ongoing debt, the U.S. government has developed some fairly useful investments for many different types of individuals. All the interest due on these securities is exempt from state and local taxes. Some, such as treasury bills, are extremely safe, liquid, and marketable but require a fair amount of cash outlay. Others, such as series EE savings bonds, can be purchased with the utmost of ease for as little as $50. It seems reasonable, then, that in today's turbulent financial climate U.S. government securities are worthy of serious examination.

7

Life Insurance

Two of every three adult Americans carry life insurance. In fact, Americans spend over 20 percent of their savings on life insurance.[1] Moreover, we spend more money on it and know less about it than any other consumer purchase. Why? Because life insurance is presented to the American public as a semimystical product basically beyond our comprehension. We are told that we cannot possibly understand its underlying principles but that if we do not make the "obvious" (obvious to the insurance agent, that is) decisions concerning it, our children, parents, spouses, and even other loved ones will suffer.

Thus we entrust our insurance needs to salespeople (they prefer to be called "advisers") who, through the use of various mysterious formulas and computer programs (the resulting printouts look magnificent, are printed in indelible ink, and, of course, must be correct), come up with exactly the right amount and type of life insurance to meet our specific needs. But the truth is that life insur-

---

[1]James H. Hunt, *How to Save Money on Life Insurance* (Consumer Report No. 1), 1982, National Insurance Consumer Organization. This report provides an excellent discussion of life insurance.

ance *is* within our grasp and that it is indeed an important part of your financial future. Furthermore, it can be made understandable, as this chapter sets out to prove. So whether or not life insurance was recommended to you in Chapter 2, I strongly suggest that you read on. For if life insurance is not presently part of your own financial picture, it may be before too long.

As you probably already know, there are many different types of life insurance, and it is true that there is one that will be just right for you. On the other hand, the chances are, to hear your "adviser" tell it, that one type will be the type representing the highest commission for him or her. It is interesting to note, for instance, that life insurance agents receive five or six times as much commission selling whole life insurance policies as they do selling term life insurance policies. Both of these, of course, will be defined as we move on. For now, though, can you guess what type I am going to recommend?

Who Needs Life Insurance?

Whether you need life insurance at all and if so, how much, should be the basic questions with which we approach the subject.

If you're single and have no dependents, you probably need little or none at all, since no one would suffer the loss of your financial contribution in the event of your death. You might want to have a small amount of insurance for what is euphemistically called your "final expenses"—a burial, a funeral, etc.—but these costs may just not be on your list of things to worry about, especially if you're relatively young. If that's the case, I recommend that you forget about wasting money on life insurance.

This, however, is not the way an insurance agent would see it, and, in fact, this group—young, single, and having no dependents—is often the target of a rather strong sales campaign. Two sales pitches are used. One is that if you start paying for your policy now, you won't have to worry about high premiums in your later years. This is true, but would you consider buying your two-year-old son a car just so you won't have to worry about the expense when he turned eighteen? The second approach is to convince a twenty-five-year-old prospective client, for instance, that he or she will not be allowed to purchase a policy later on in life at the ripe old age of thirty or thirty-five and thus will have to bear the ultimate disgrace of being uninsurable. Sure it's a possibility, but a highly unlikely one, even at the age of forty.

For a married couple without children in which both spouses work and earn comparable salaries, insurance might be needed, but even here, needs would be limited. For if one spouse should die, their savings, plus the salary of the survivor, probably would be sufficient to cover financial needs.

On the other hand, for a childless married couple in which one spouse is earning considerably more than the other, insurance would be recommended for the higher wage-earner, since his or her death could definitely leave the other at a loss.

Where life insurance is needed the most is precisely where it is least affordable. That is the married couple with children or with dependent parents with one or both spouses working. Here is where a substantial amount of insurance is definitely needed. It is also the situation in which current expenses are the greatest (supporting a home, paying for kids' educational needs, and so on) relative to current income. This is the group that will benefit the most from this chapter.

Other than this group described above, most people carry too much life insurance, which is a reflection on the marvelous job our insurance "advisers" have done. Excess insurance is most often carried by people in their fifties and beyond whose children are grown and financially independent, whose mortgages have been paid off, and whose savings nest egg would most likely cover their expenses after death. Generally, these people need only a limited amount of insurance, especially when you look at the fact that 95 percent of all estates involve little or no taxes (now most estates are too small to be taxed to any great degree) and that there are no taxes due whatsoever if all estate proceeds are passed on to the surviving spouse.[2]

An important rule of thumb to remember is that children do not need their own lives insured, but parents do to protect their children's futures. Again, it's another superlative commentary on the life insurance industry as a whole that large numbers of children under the age of twelve are covered by life insurance policies. These policies were sold to parents who were convinced that it was the only way they could help their children's futures. If that is your intention (and it is, by all means, admirable), instead of paying annual, often unreasonable, premiums on such policies, invest $2,000 instead for your child and let that money grow. In twenty years it will be worth approximately $30,000.[3] Of course, if you do decide to make this investment instead of taking out a life insurance policy on your child, don't tell your insurance agent about it; he or she is likely to get *extremely* upset.

Term Life Insurance vs. Whole Life Insurance

Before we move on to a discussion of how much insurance you need, it is important to understand exactly why I strongly recommend term life policies over whole life policies.

The type of insurance that most people have (although, happily, this is changing rapidly) is whole life, also known as straight life or ordinary life insurance. This is the type of insurance that requires you to make annual, semiannual, or quarterly payments that remain the same for the entire

---

[2]This provision is contained in the Tax Equity and Fiscal Responsibility Act of 1982.

[3]Assuming you invest it at a fixed 12 percent annual rate of return using any of the appropriate vehicles mentioned in this book. If you obtain only a 10 percent annual return, the money will be worth $24,000 in twenty years. At a 15 percent return it will grow to a total of $43,000.

life of the policy. After a number of years, usually ten, your policy begins developing a fairly substantial *cash value*—that is, your policy is worth a sum of money that you can borrow against even before your demise.[4] Now, that may sound like a pretty good deal, but if you've gotten this far in this book and have been reading thoroughly, you should already know that there is no such thing as a free lunch.[5]

Here's how that policy works: A thirty-five-year-old male purchases a $100,000 whole life policy. His annual premium is approximately $2,000 (see Table 1). After ten years, when he's reached the age of forty-five, the cash value of his policy is approximately $21,500 (see Table 2).

Now let's double back and take a closer look at that "investment," for that is precisely how this policy was pitched.

Whole life insurance actually has two components, neither of which is generally spelled out. One is the insurance end of it. If the individual in the above example should die, his beneficiary would receive $100,000. The insurance component, the part of the premium that pays for the $100,000 benefit, actually is a small part of the $2,000 annual premium, perhaps no more than $250.[6]

The second part of that insurance premium is the investment portion. Thus, out of a $2,000 annual premium, $250 of it is used to pay for the insurance portion of the coverage, while the other $1,750 is invested for you. *Part of the returns on that investment becomes the cash value of the policy.* And guess what your average return is on that $1,750 annual investment. It's 5 to 6 percent.[7]

Now, it's likely that this bit of news causes you to raise a few questions. For instance, haven't they ever heard of

---

[4]Chapter 3 explains how to borrow against the cash value of an insurance policy.

[5]As Professor Milton Friedman, Nobel Laureate, has often said.

[6]The insurance company figures out the exact ratio through the use of actuarial or probability tables showing the chances of our thirty-five-year-old dying before his thirty-sixth birthday.

[7]From a recent Federal Trade Commission report.

Table 1.
Annual Premium Cost of Term vs. Whole Life Insurance*

| Age† | $10,000 coverage | | $50,000 coverage | | $100,000 coverage | |
	Term‡	Whole Life	Term	Whole Life	Term	Whole Life
25	$ 19–40	$128–167	$ 87–198	$ 640–833	$ 195–396	$1,280–1,666
30	19–41	148–192	87–203	740–960	195–406	1,480–1,921
35	24–46	175–226	122–232	870–1,130	245–465	1,740–2,260
40	36–60	210–267	182–304	1,050–1,349	365–608	2,100–2,699
45	55–84	259–327	277–420	1,295–1,633	555–840	2,590–3,267
50	86–122	328–401	432–604	1,640–2,005	865–1,219	3,280–4,010
55	135–180	399–499	675–904	1,995–2,495	1,350–1,809	3,990–4,993
60	211–273	532–631	1,055–1,363	2,662–3,155	2,110–2,725	5,324–6,310

*Based on the cost per $1,000 of coverage for sample higher- and lower-priced policies.
†Cost shown for males.
‡Five-year renewable convertible term.

Source: From Everyone's Money Book by Jane Bryant Quinn. Copyright © 1979 by Jane Bryant Quinn. Reprinted by permission of Delacorte Press.

money market funds or government securities or a host of other higher-paying investments that will be covered later in this book? The answer is not important. What is important is that *you* have heard of these, and you could make a lot more for your money than a paltry 5 or 6 percent, couldn't you?

Look at it this way: When you buy auto insurance, for the years you don't have an accident you get nothing, not even a thank-you note from the insurance company. Nor do you expect anything. And after years of paying for this insurance, you would hardly expect to have, say, $5,000 available to you in cash value. So why, then, should you expect to have it after years of paying for an insurance policy? Remember, though, cash value is possible only if you give the insurance company that extra money to invest for you, for cash value is the return on your *invested* funds.

Table 2.
Saving in a Straight-Life Policy vs. Saving Elsewhere*
(Based on a $100,000 Insurance Policy)

	Starting at Age 25			Starting at Age 35		
Age	Cash value in Straight-life Policy†	Savings at 8%‡	Savings at 10%‡	Cash value in Straight-life Policy†	Savings at 8%‡	Savings at 10%‡
30	$ 5,370	$ 7,540	$ 7,982			
35	15,210	18,618	20,862			
40	28,320§	34,572	41,264	$ 7,770	$ 10,892	$ 11,545
45	46,090§	57,257	73,341	21,490	26,132	29,338
50	69,900§	89,369	123,726	39,420	47,315	56,726
55	101,600§	134,577	202,814	63,230	76,469	98,766
60	143,390§	197,881	326,974	94,500	116,223	163,235
65	196,970§	286,094	521,886	134,590	168,098	262,736

*With thanks to William Ardito and Scott Beckley, William G. Ardito Associates.

†Projected cash values, using dividends to buy additional paid-up insurance.

‡Net return after taxes, no matter what the bracket.

§These numbers are all overstated, because they're before-tax returns. At this point, the cash value is higher than the premiums paid. The policyholder would subtract the premiums from the cash value and pay income taxes on the difference.

Note: This table shows the savings buildup in a straight-life policy compared with buying term insurance and investing the difference. A *low-cost* straight-life policy was used for the illustration; higher-cost policies would show up more poorly.

Source: From *Everyone's Money Book* by Jane Bryant Quinn. Copyright © 1979 by Jane Bryant Quinn. Reprinted by permission of Delacorte Press.

This, basically, is how whole life insurance policies work. Their inflated premiums and the poor investments that are made on your behalf cause me to recommend against them so strongly.

But, of course, if you speak to an insurance adviser about these matters, this is precisely the policy he or she will try to sell you, for on a $100,000 whole life policy for a thirty-five-year-old individual, the agent commission for the first year of that policy (the agent's commission is broken down somewhat over the first few years of the life of the policy) is approximately $900, as opposed to a $100 commission on a term policy. And this, of course, is the reason that these policies are sold so diligently. Let's face it: If you were an insurance agent, which one would you favor? Sure, you'd have ethics, but you'd have a family to support, too, wouldn't you?

Consider also this piece of startling information: Within the first two years after a whole life policy has been purchased, *when little or no cash value has accrued*, 20 percent of these policies are dropped, and by the time ten years have elapsed, about 50 percent are dropped.[8]

What happens is that the policyholders discover—too late, of course—that their insurance needs can be met more cheaply through other types of insurance. The resulting losses in misspent investment dollars, by this time, are staggering. The policies that most of these people turn to and that finally are gaining popularity among the bulk of new policyholders is term life insurance.

Put very simply, term insurance is pure insurance. You purchase a term policy so that your beneficiary receives a sum of money in the event of your untimely death. That's it. There's no cash surrender value; you can't ever borrow against it. It's simple life insurance, and because of its simplicity, it is the cheapest insurance around. And as you already know, it's the type I recommend—with no exception—to anyone needing life insurance.

The Hidden Costs in Whole Life Insurance Policies

One of the things an insurance agent might tell you when trying to sell a whole life policy over a term policy is that whole life premiums remain the same throughout the life of the policy, whereas with term insurance, the premiums start with a lower premium that then goes up over

---

[8]James H. Hunt, *How to Save Money on Life Insurance* (Consumer Report No. 1), 1982, National Insurance Consumer Organization.

the years. So even though whole life premiums start out much higher, as the agent would put it, they at least remain constant. What they then tell you, *and it's true*, is that term insurance gets more expensive as you get older. What they don't tell you is that the same is true of whole life insurance as well. But in this case the increasing costs—and the real facts—are well hidden. Here's how they work it.

With a whole life policy, when you die, the insurance company must pay only the difference between the cash value accrued (that is, a portion of the investment component of the premium you have been paying) and the face value of the policy. Your beneficiary, of course, gets the face value of the policy, but you have actually already paid a portion of that face value. If you bought the policy recently and little or no cash value has accrued, the insurance company must put up a larger chunk of money toward that death benefit. But if you've been carrying the policy for many years and have built up a large cash value, you actually wind up contributing more money toward that death benefit, and the insurance company, which must make up the difference, contributes less. Thus, as time goes by and your contribution adds up, the insurance company's contribution, or liability, decreases. You're actually getting less insurance for the same premium. Thus, the whole life policy *is* getting more expensive, just as it does with a term policy.

This is probably the most complicated aspect of insurance, and my clients often have trouble grasping it at first. But it's crucial that you understand it before an insurance agent ever comes to visit you.

Table 3 should help you to examine how all this works. It illustrates a $100,000 whole life policy purchased by a twenty-five-year-old male. The annual premium is constant, at $1,670 a year. Note that as the numbers in the cash value column increase, the portion of the death benefit that the insurance company must provide decreases. The point here is that as the policyholder gets older, the actual cost of each $10,000 worth of protection goes up.

Table 3.
The Rising Cost of Protection Under a $100,000 Straight Life Insurance Policy

Age	Annual Premium	Cash Value	Insurance Company Liability	Actual Cost Per $10,000 of Protection
25	$1,670	0	$100,000	$167.00
30	1,670	$ 4,900	95,100	175.80
35	1,670	12,700	87,300	191.30
40	1,670	20,000	80,000	208.70
45	1,670	27,900	72,100	231.90

In an excellent book on the insurance industry, Andrew Tobias discusses the deficient rate of return on whole life policies, especially of those policies held for less than ten years.[9] As Table 4 so vividly demonstrates, it is possible to obtain a negative rate of return on such a policy. Other than in the case of savings bank life insurance, which will be discussed briefly later, the best rate of return was on a policy held for twenty-nine years, and even then the return was a mere 6.45 percent—and that was the best!

Table 5 presents the recommendations of the National Insurance Consumer Organization (NICO), which amounts to purchasing one-year renewable term insurance. It shows the rates per $1,000 of life insurance for smokers and nonsmokers, and I've included those figures just in case you needed another good reason to stop smoking; the premiums for smokers are, for obvious reasons, higher. One other item of interest also becomes apparent: Women's premiums are lower, since women have tended, on the average, to live longer. It will be interesting to note whether this disparity in premium costs will change as more women join the work force.

Both Massachusetts and New York State offer savings

---

[9]Andrew Tobias, *The Invisible Bankers* (New York: Simon & Schuster), 1981. See especially Chapter 14.

Table 4.
Sample Whole Life Yields

Company/Policy	Yield on Savings Element if Held for:			Annual Premium
	9 years	19 years	29 years	
$25,000 Nonparticipating policies				
Allstate Life Executive Plan, age 25				
nonsmoker	0.03%	3.99%	3.98%	$ 249
smoker	-0.63%	3.69%	3.78%	$ 254
Travelers Ordinary Life, age 25	0.93%	3.61%	3.14%	$ 293
Connecticut General Ordinary Life, age 25	-6.04%	1.75%	2.28%	$ 309
Aetna Whole Life, age 35	-1.27%	2.86%	3.19%	$ 392
J. C. Penney Value Select, age 45	-0.50%	2.91%	3.33%	$ 575
Hartford Life Whole Life, age 45	-1.89%	2.13%	2.79%	$ 613
$25,000 Participating Policies				
Massachusetts SBLI, age 25*	8.54%	7.97%	7.85%	$ 236
New England Mutual, age 25*	3.64%	6.26%	6.45%	$ 296
Massachusetts Mutual Convertible Life, age 25*	3.40%	5.98%	6.08%	$ 302
Prudential, Modified Life 3, age 25	1.20%	4.91%	5.40%	$ 400

New York Life, age 25	2.23%	5.10%	5.54%	$ 374
John Hancock Paid Up at 85, age 25	-1.75%	3.74%	4.68%	$ 394
Equitable Adjusted Whole Life, age 35	1.66%	4.85%	5.27%	$ 526
$100,000 Participating Policies				
Northwestern Mutual, age 25*	2.58%	5.36%	5.98%	$1,411
Equitable Adjusted Whole Life, age 25	1.98%	5.15%	5.55%	$1,445
Metropolitan Life, Whole Life, age 25	-2.60%	4.03%	5.06%	$1,272
Phoenix Mutual, nonsmokers, age 35*	3.26%	5.78%	5.94%	$2,062
Franklin Life Executive Select II, age 35	-1.70%	3.44%	4.22%	$2,272
Manhattan Life Challenger, age 35	-1.02%	3.58%	4.15%	$2,316
Prudential Estate 20, Whole Life, age 35	0.24%	3.99%	4.79%	$2,043
State Farm "Estate Protector" (L95), age 45	0.31%	4.29%	4.56%	$2,542
State Farm Whole Life, age 45	-1.56%	3.59%	4.40%	$3,048

*Based on a sampling of evaluations by Consumers Union of several hundred life insurance policies. See *The Consumer Union Report on Life Insurance*, fourth edition.

Source: From *The Invisible Bankers* by Andrew Tobias. Reprinted by permission of Linden Press, a Simon & Schuster division of Gulf & Western Corporation.

bank life insurance (SBLI). Over the years, these policies have proved to be among the most reasonably priced and offer the best returns on your insurance funds (see Table 4). The policies are available only in these two states, and both have restrictions as to who may purchase the policies based on certain residency and employment requirements. Also, the maximum amounts of the policies are limited. In New York State, the savings banks have consistently tried to raise the $30,000 limit, but opposition from the life insurance industry has proved too strong.

The following list represents further recommendations of NICO—that is, reputable insurance companies that have fairly low insurance rates. Although NICO's list of best bets actually includes over a hundred companies, I have for the most part listed those that additionally offer lower rates for nonsmokers.

Allstate
(available through
any Sears store)

Berkshire Life Insurance Company
700 South Street
Pittsfield, MA 01201
(413)499-4321

Central Life Assurance Company
Box 1555
Des Moines, IA 50306
(515)283-2371

Columbia Mutual Insurance Company
Box 618
Columbia, MO 65205
(314)474-6193

Connecticut Mutual Life Insurance
140 Garden Street
Hartford, CT 06115
(203)727-6500

Country Life Insurance
1701 Towonda Avenue
Bloomington, IL 61701
(309)557-2111

Empire General Life Insurance
600 South Lake
Pasadena, CA 91106
(213)792-2096

Federal Home Life Insurance
78 West Michigan Mall
Battle Creek, MI 49017
(616)968-5500

Fidelity Union Life
P.O. Box 500
Bradford, PA 19101
(215)964-7000

Great Southern Life Insurance
3121 Buffalo Speedway
Houston, TX 77098
(713)622-2000

Gulf Life Insurance Company
1301 Gulf Life Drive
Jacksonville, FL 32207
(904)390-7000

Home Life Insurance Company
253 Broadway
New York, NY 10007
(212)306-2000

Jackson National Life Insurance Company
5901 Executive Drive
Lansing, MI 48909
(517)394-3400

Massachusetts Mutual Life Insurance
1295 State Street
Springfield, MA 01111
(413)788-8411

Metropolitan Life Insurance Company
1 Madison Avenue
New York, NY 10019
(212)578-2211

Northwestern Mutual Life Insurance Company
720 East Wisconsin Avenue
Milwaukee, WI 53202
(414)271-1444

Pacific Mutual Life Insurance
700 Newport Center Drive
Newport Beach, CA 92660
(714)640-3011

Phoenix Mutual Life Insurance Company
1 American Row
Hartford, CT 06115
(203)278-1212

Prudential Insurance Company of America
Prudential Plaza
Newark, NJ 07101
(201)877-6000

Standard Insurance Company
1100 SW Sixth Avenue
Portland, OR 97204
(503)248-2700

You are now armed with a good understanding of how insurance policies work, and if you've read carefully, you should be ready to do battle with any fast-talking insurance agent who might come your way. In fact, you have all the basic pieces of information you'll need, except one.

How Much Insurance Do You Need?

The important thing to remember about the amount of insurance you take out is that you are purchasing it so that your surviving dependents will be provided with an income in case of your death. Your aim is to make provisions whereby they will be able to go on living much as they are currently. Generally speaking, if you can provide them with 70 to 80 percent of your current take-home pay through insurance *and all other sources of income available to them,* you will have made sufficient provisions. Bear in mind that your insurance need not cover all the funds needed, for other sources of money will be available to them.

Until the laws change, a good portion of the income might be available through Social Security benefits, which are tax-free. As of this writing, a widow with one or more dependents, for instance, is entitled to annual benefits of from $5,000 to about $14,400.[10] Before you can determine the amount of insurance you need, you must contact your local Social Security office (consult the white pages) to find out exactly what the benefits will be. You must also find out how many years your family will be eligible for those benefits. This sum will help to satisfy part of the 70 to 80 percent of your after-tax income that you are seeking to replace.

Thus, if you are currently earning $36,000 a year and taking home $27,000, your family needs an annual income of 70 to 80 percent of that, or $18,900 to $21,600.

The amount of insurance you need to provide is further reduced by the sum of your present assets and any income that the family may easily provide for itself. As you use the step-by-step formula on pages 112–113 for determining the exact size of your policy, you will be asked to find out whether you have stocks, bonds, and other assets that your family can easily sell. Determine these by reviewing

---

[10]The maximum Social Security benefit for a widow with one or more children is approximately $1,200 a month.

Table 5.
NICO-Recommended Maximum Term Rates Per $1,000 of Life Insurance Protection

MEN

Age	Nonsmokers			Smokers		
	$50,000	$100,000	$250,000	$50,000	$100,000	$250,000
25 and under	$ 2.16	$ 1.76	$ 1.52	$ 2.50	$ 2.10	$ 1.86
26	2.18	1.78	1.54	2.52	2.12	1.88
27	2.19	1.79	1.55	2.54	2.14	1.90
28	2.21	1.81	1.57	2.56	2.16	1.92
29	2.22	1.82	1.58	2.58	2.18	1.94
30	2.24	1.84	1.60	2.60	2.20	1.96
31	2.26	1.86	1.62	2.62	2.22	1.98
32	2.27	1.87	1.63	2.64	2.24	2.00
33	2.30	1.90	1.66	2.68	2.28	2.04
34	2.34	1.94	1.70	2.72	2.32	2.08
35	2.40	2.00	1.76	2.80	2.40	2.16
36	2.50	2.10	1.86	2.92	2.52	2.28
37	2.61	2.21	1.97	3.06	2.66	2.42
38	2.72	2.32	2.08	3.20	2.80	2.56
39	2.85	2.45	2.21	3.36	2.96	2.72
40	2.98	2.58	2.34	3.53	3.13	2.89

41	3.14	2.74	2.50	3.72	3.32	3.08
42	3.35	2.95	2.71	3.99	3.59	3.35
43	3.58	3.18	2.94	4.28	3.88	3.64
44	3.84	3.44	3.20	4.60	4.20	3.96
45	4.14	3.74	3.50	4.98	4.58	4.34
46	4.16	4.06	3.82	5.37	4.97	4.73
47	4.80	4.40	4.16	5.80	5.40	5.16
48	5.17	4.77	4.53	6.26	5.86	5.62
49	5.60	5.20	4.96	6.80	6.40	6.16
50	6.06	5.66	5.42	7.37	6.97	6.73
51	6.58	6.18	5.94	8.02	7.62	7.38
52	7.14	6.74	6.50	8.72	8.32	8.08
53	7.74	7.34	7.10	9.48	9.08	8.84
54	8.42	8.02	7.78	10.33	9.93	9.69
55	9.18	8.78	8.54	11.23	10.88	10.64
56	10.03	9.63	9.39	12.34	11.94	11.70
57	10.96	10.56	10.32	13.50	13.10	12.86
58	11.98	11.58	11.34	14.78	14.38	14.14
59	13.10	12.70	12.46	16.18	15.78	15.54
60	14.24	13.84	13.60	17.60	17.20	16.96
61	15.39	14.99	14.75	19.04	18.64	18.40
62	16.78	16.38	16.14	20.78	20.38	20.14
63	18.43	18.03	17.79	22.84	22.44	22.20
64	20.32	19.92	19.68	25.20	24.80	24.56
65	22.48	22.08	21.84	27.90	27.50	27.26

NICO-Recommended Maximum Term Rates Per $1,000 of Life Insurance Protection

WOMEN

Age	Nonsmokers			Smokers		
	$50,000	$100,000	$250,000	$50,000	$100,000	$250,000
25 and under	$ 2.10	$ 1.70	$ 1.46	$ 2.43	$ 2.03	$ 1.79
26	2.11	1.71	1.47	2.44	2.04	1.80
27	2.13	1.73	1.49	2.46	2.06	1.82
28	2.14	1.74	1.50	2.48	2.08	1.84
29	2.16	1.76	1.52	2.50	2.10	1.86
30	2.18	1.78	1.54	2.52	2.12	1.88
31	2.19	1.79	1.55	2.54	2.14	1.90
32	2.21	1.81	1.57	2.56	2.16	1.92
33	2.22	1.82	1.58	2.58	2.18	1.94
34	2.24	1.84	1.60	2.60	2.20	1.96
35	2.26	1.86	1.62	2.62	2.22	1.98
36	2.28	1.88	1.64	2.65	2.25	2.01
37	2.31	1.91	1.67	2.69	2.29	2.05
38	2.34	1.94	1.70	2.73	2.33	2.09
39	2.42	2.02	1.78	2.82	2.42	2.18
40	2.51	2.11	1.87	2.94	2.54	2.30

108

41	2.43	2.67	3.07	1.98	2.22	2.62
42	2.57	2.81	3.21	2.09	2.33	2.73
43	2.73	2.97	3.37	2.22	2.46	2.86
44	2.90	3.14	3.54	2.35	2.59	2.99
45	3.08	3.32	3.72	2.50	2.74	3.14
46	3.34	3.58	3.98	2.70	2.94	3.34
47	3.63	3.87	4.27	2.94	3.18	3.58
48	3.94	4.18	4.58	3.18	3.42	3.82
49	4.29	4.53	4.93	3.46	3.70	4.10
50	4.68	4.94	5.32	3.78	4.02	4.42
51	5.09	5.33	5.73	4.10	4.34	4.74
52	5.54	5.78	6.18	4.46	4.70	5.10
53	6.05	6.29	6.69	4.87	5.11	5.51
54	6.63	6.87	7.27	5.34	5.58	5.98
55	7.22	7.46	7.86	5.81	6.05	6.45
56	7.87	8.11	8.51	6.33	6.57	6.97
57	8.58	8.82	9.22	6.90	7.14	7.54
58	9.41	9.65	10.05	7.56	7.80	8.20
59	10.31	10.55	10.95	8.28	8.52	8.92
60	11.30	11.54	11.94	9.07	9.31	9.71
61	12.40	12.64	13.04	9.95	10.19	10.59
62	13.60	13.84	14.24	10.91	11.15	11.55
63	14.91	15.15	15.55	11.96	12.20	12.60
64	16.28	16.52	16.92	13.06	13.30	13.70
65	17.68	17.92	18.32	14.18	14.42	14.82

the list of assets you prepared in Chapter 2. Do not, however, include your home, as moving probably would pose a hardship for your family in the event of your death.

The next important question to ask is, How long will your family need that annual income? Is your spouse likely to remarry? Will your children soon be grown and be able to provide further support? Is your spouse likely to take a job that will provide adequate income for the family? If your children are very young and you cannot foresee your spouse being free to work in the near future, you may want to provide them with an income that will last over the course of twenty years after your death. But if the children are older and it seems likely that your spouse will take a job, you may want to ensure that income for only ten years.

To be sure, these questions are extremely difficult to answer, for it is often impossible to imagine what life would be like for our families after we go. On the other hand, it is very important that you take a realistic look at what is likely to occur and make your educated guess based on the events that seem most probable.

Using the example we started out with, suppose you need to replace $19,000 of your present income, and let's further suppose that Social Security will provide $9,000 of that sum. The gap you need to fill is $10,000 a year. Now let's assume that you've decided to provide your family with that amount for twenty years after your death. Your next assumption is that your family will invest that money so that the interest it earns will further provide some of the funds needed. (Make a copy of this book part of your estate!) Table 6 shows how an insurance benefit, invested at various rates of interest, provides needed income over various time periods. For instance, to provide your survivors with $10,000 a year for twenty years, assuming the money will be invested at a rate of 9 percent (compounded), a lump sum of approximately $93,000 is needed. To provide a $15,000 annuity for thirty years, assuming the money could be invested at only a 6 percent rate of return, the sum needed would be $210,000.

Table 6.
The Amount of Funds Needed to Provide Various Levels of Annual Income over a Ten-, Twenty-, or Thirty-Year Period

Annual Income Needed	Assumed Annual Investment Return*	10 Years	20 Years	30 Years
$5,000	6%	$ 38,000	$ 59,000	$ 70,000
($417 per month)	9%	33,000	47,000	55,000
	10%	32,000	44,000	48,000
	12%	29,000	38,000	41,000
$10,000	6%	76,000	117,000	140,000
($833 per month)	9%	66,000	93,000	104,000
	10%	64,000	87,000	96,000
	12%	59,000	77,000	82,000
$15,000	6%	113,000	175,000	210,000
($1,250 per month)	9%	100,000	135,000	157,000
	10%	95,000	131,000	144,000
	12%	88,000	115,000	123,000
$18,000	6%	136,000	210,000	251,000
($1,500 per month)	9%	120,000	168,000	188,000
	10%	115,000	157,000	172,000
	12%	106,000	138,000	147,000
$24,000	6%	181,000	281,000	335,000
($2,000 per month)	9%	159,000	224,000	250,000
	10%	153,000	209,000	230,000
	12%	141,000	184,000	196,000

*These calculations assume that interest is compounded monthly.

Reading the table in this way, you can find the lump sum of money needed for your family's specific needs. Bear in mind, though, that these numbers do not represent the amount of insurance you need; we'll get to that in a moment. If some of the resulting numbers from Table 6 seem a bit low to you, remember that your heirs will be in a much lower tax bracket than you are currently in since Social Security payments are tax-free and the remaining income will be taxed at a lower rate.

Take time to look at the table now to find the sum of money needed for the income you seek to replace over the period you've decided on. Now use the following steps to determine what the face value of your life insurance ought to be.[11]

STEP 1
Figure out what your annual take-home pay is and then multiply that by 70 to 80 percent.   _____

STEP 2
Find out what your family's annual Social Security benefit would be if you died today. _____

STEP 3
Subtotal of steps 1 and 2. (Subtract the sum in step 2 from the sum in step 1.)   _____

STEP 4
Determine the approximate sum of money needed to cover this amount over the number of years you've decided you'd like to provide that benefit. (Consult Table 6.)   _____

STEP 5
Estimate the cost of your final expenses, including funeral and burial costs, any debts that might have to be paid, etc. Generally, these come to about 50 percent of your current annual take-home pay.   _____

---

[11]These steps are based on Andrew Tobias' fine system as described in *The Invisible Bankers*.

STEP 6
Add the totals in steps 4 and 5. This gives you the *maximum* amount of life insurance coverage you need. _____

STEP 7
Estimate the value of other assets you may have, such as stocks, bonds, pensions, profit-sharing interests, life insurance policies held through employers, etc. (Consult the list of assets you prepared in Chapter 2. Do not include the value of your home, since you do not want to force your family to move.) _____

STEP 8
Estimate the sum of any other income your family may have access to, such as income from a job held by your spouse, contributions from wealthy grandparents, and any substantial items that your family would probably sell, such as a boat, a second car, etc. _____

STEP 9
Add the totals in steps 7 and 8. _____

STEP 10
Subtract the total in step 9 from the total in step 6. This is the amount of life insurance you need. _____

By using the above formula, you can come up with a very reasonable approximation of your current life insurance needs. But remember that circumstances change. Your salary may rise substantially over the next few years, your investments may yield a high profit, you may even be the beneficiary of a large inheritance. A birth, death, or marriage in the family could change the picture further.

Furthermore, Social Security laws do change, and you must stay on top of these changes. The point to remember here is that your insurance needs should be reviewed annually, and your policy should be adjusted accordingly. There are few things sadder than a family trying to survive on insurance benefits that were calculated on needs that were last assessed ten years before the demise of the major wage-earner.

Hopefully, by this point, the subject of life insurance has been somewhat demystified. To be sure, the subject is vast; lengthy volumes have been filled with its ins and outs. What you have been given, however, are the basics that underlie the structure of the life insurance game. No doubt, as you attempt to do business with agents and representatives, you will encounter new terms and new concepts, for as with any other area of financial planning, things change constantly as the corporate powers that be attempt to stay one step ahead of public needs—or one step behind, depending on how you look at it. And, as with any other area of financial planning, you have a right to understand it all. Once again, demand reasonable answers to your questions before you decide to do business with any one company. And above all, shop around. Premiums on comparable policies can vary as much as 100 percent.

If you do run into a problem with a company once you have taken out a policy, there are a number of things you can do after you have established that the company itself will give you no satisfaction. You can contact your state insurance department by calling your state capital and asking for the proper address and phone number. (The insurance industry is regulated by the individual state governments, not the federal government.) Or you might try writing to the insurance industry's trade association, the American Council of Life Insurance, 1850 K Street NW, Washington, DC 20006. Be sure to keep copies of all correspondence.

8

Real Estate

During the past decade, real-estate investments have proved to be among the best available. That is, home ownership especially (as opposed to real-estate funds, which are not recommended in this book) has proved to be a wise choice for a large sector of the population due to a myriad of governmental inducements available and a little help from inflation.

In this chapter we will discuss why home ownership (including one- and two-family dwellings as well as cooperatives and condominiums) is definitely advised as a favorable life-style choice, as an advantageous long-term investment, and as a more than reasonable tax shelter, for it has come to the point, in the 1980s, where the government's generosity actually helps you pay for your humble abode.

Why Purchase a Home?

Before the investment and tax-shelter reasons for purchasing a home are discussed, there is one critical reason that must underlie all others, and this would be your desire to

115

live in a particular home and in the neighborhood you have chosen. This is paramount, for regardless of the other economic incentives that will be put forth shortly, no one can guarantee that your home will prove a good investment over the long run nor that the tax laws will not change in the future. It would be sad, indeed, if you purchased a home solely or mostly as an investment and then found out that you disliked living in it. You might console yourself by saying, "At least it was a good investment," but what if that home did not rise in value, as you had anticipated? You would have lost out on the pleasure of a residence you could enjoy as well as the economic advantages.

Thus, the primary reason for your real-estate purchase should be your wanting to live there. Probably—and hopefully—the investment components of your decision will come through as well.

As far as your home purchase is concerned, the government really is your ally, and it is forever trying to accommodate you in this respect. Why? Because the government believes that homeowners, as opposed to renters, will benefit the communities, as more involved citizens. Put another way, homeowners have their equity at stake, and the government feels that as a result, they will do all they can to guard it by taking care of their property and through civic and social involvement. Furthermore, as we'll see, it's a better situation for the national economy.

How does the government help? First of all, it makes all mortgage interest payments tax-deductible. This is a biggie, since 90 percent of the mortgage payments you make for the first five years constitute interest. Thus, if you're making monthly mortgage payments of $700 (or $8,400 annually), over $600 of that, which would make up the interest portion of the payment, is tax-deductible.

The second gift from Uncle Sam is that *all* real-estate taxes are also tax-deductible. So if your real-estate taxes are $2,000 a year, all of it is deductible on your tax return.

You might argue that those two "gifts" are only fair. Not so, for in the case of the first, it should be remembered that in most parts of the world, including Canada, mortgage interest payments are *not* tax-deductible. As far as the second benefit is concerned, some might say that all taxes are tax-deductible and thus so should real-estate taxes be. But that's not true, for Social Security contributions are actually taxes, and they are *not* tax-deductible. In addition, gasoline taxes, which were once deductible, no longer are. (The government giveth, and the government taketh away.)

Using the example cited above, where there was an annual mortgage payment of $8,400 and an annual real-estate tax of $2,000, the government would regard over 90 percent of the former (or about $7,500) and 100 percent of the latter as admissible tax-deductible expenses. The exact tax savings to you, of course, depend upon your tax bracket. For instance, if you are in the 30 percent tax bracket, that monthly $867 cost really winds up being $628. That's a tax saving of over $200 monthly or $2,868 annually.[1] As your tax bracket goes up, so do your savings. In the 50 percent tax bracket, your monthly costs dwindle to $468 monthly, affording you an annual savings of over $4,700. When you're calculating the cost of home ownership, always remember to do your calculations using net amounts after taxes.

Fine, you might say. The real monthly cost on an $867 payment is only $548 after taxes, but you still can't afford to shell out the $867 a month. Assuming you *can* afford the $548, there is something you can do to reduce the monthly payment, and this is to get your employer to increase your tax deductions to reflect your mortgage interest payments and real-estate taxes. This will reduce your weekly withholding tax, which will result in greater take-home pay. It will also reduce your tax refund, for in effect you will have received the money over the course of the year.

What this will do is increase your deductions by roughly

---

[1]See Appendix A, "How Your Income Is Taxed," for a complete discussion of how this works.

117

the equivalent of one dependent for each $1,000 of additional tax deductions. Thus, $9,560 of new deductions would translate into the equivalent of eight or nine new dependents. Of course, this example is given for calculation purposes only. When you file your tax return on April 15, you will, of course, enter the proper number of dependents and also include the real-estate tax and mortgage-interest cost in their proper places as tax-deductible expenses.

Now we have seen how an $867 monthly cost could be reduced to $548. But the continuing saga of how the government seduces you into buying a home (notwithstanding recent high interest rates) does not end there.

The government further sweetens the pot by instituting a perpetual deferment on the capital gain from the sale of your home. If you buy any other asset, such as a stock or a bond, and sell it at a profit, you must pay taxes on the proceeds. As we've already seen elsewhere in this book, if the asset is held for more than one year, you are charged the lower capital-gains rate. If the asset is held for less than one year, you are charged the normal income-tax rate. But your home, *if it is your principal residence,* is not like any other asset. New (and better) rules for you come into play here. Here's how they work:

If you bought a house in 1972 for $35,000 and sell it today for $75,000, you make a $40,000 capital gains profit. For any other asset, your normal tax on that sale could be as high as $8,000. But not for your humble abode, for if you buy another home within two years for as much or more than the one you sold, the government says you can *defer all taxes.* Thus you can save $8,000 just because Uncle Sam would like you to buy another home. Of course, if you decided not to buy and rent something instead, you would have to pay up to $8,000 in capital gains taxes immediately. But if this is not the case, you can defer that tax payment indefinitely as long as you remain a homeowner. In the event of your death, your estate would settle the tab with Uncle Sam.

So far we have seen the government benefits of tax

118

deductions and tax deferments. But now we have come to the ultimate advantage—*no taxes at all*! I call it the $125,000 Special, and it works like this: If you or your spouse is fifty-five years old or older and has lived in your primary residence for at least three of the past five years, you pay *no* taxes on up to $125,000 of the profit from the sale of that home. A sample scenario helps to point out the true beauty of this benefit.

Suppose that as a struggling couple back in 1957, you and your spouse purchased a home for the enormous sum of—or at least it seemed so back then—$14,000. In 1970 you sold that house for $40,000 and paid no taxes on the $26,000 profit, since you immediately purchased another for $40,000. In 1983 you are fifty-six years old. The children have grown, and your four-bedroom Tudor is much too large for you and your spouse, so you sell it for a whopping $114,000. But your good fortune does not end with the profit you've made, for Uncle Sam has smiled on you: *You pay no taxes and pocket the full $114,000!* This is what might best be referred to, as far as real estate is concerned, as the new math. You started out paying $14,000 for a home and wind up with a profit of $100,000. By invoking the $125,000 Special, it is all tax-free. Had that benefit not been available to you, you would have wound up paying as much as $20,000 in taxes.

Note that once you have drawn on the $125,000 Special tax benefit, even if you have not fully used the $125,000, you cannot use the remainder. The offer is good only for one time per family. If you and your spouse get divorced after you have used it, neither of you will be entitled to utilize it again.[2]

Prior to July 1981, this benefit went up to only $100,000. There is no doubt in my mind that in the near future it will be raised to $150,000 and that by the end of this decade it is most likely to be known as the $200,000 Special.

---

[2] If this is your situation and you decide to remarry, you might want to know whether your new spouse has ever invoked the $125,000 Special.

What You Can Expect from the Real-Estate Market

As I mentioned at the outset of this chapter, no one can guarantee that the value of the house you buy will increase. On the other hand, most real estate has gone up in value over the past years, and a look at that trend might be useful here.

In Chart 1 we see the median sales prices of existing (not new) single-family homes for the month of March for the years 1976 through 1982. The chart shows a continuous increase in values, from $37,200 in 1976 to $67,200 in 1982. This represents an 81 percent increase over the seven-year period, quite respectable indeed considering that most real estate is leveraged, which simply means that you buy it with only some of your money and a lot of other people's money (that is, a bank's, through a mortgage).

Consider this: If you purchased the mythical average home in 1976 for $37,200 by applying an $8,000 down payment and a $29,000 mortgage, your total return on the investment would *not* have been the 81 percent increase but closer to 475 percent, or 25 percent a year compounded, since you really started out by investing only $8,000 in cash.

The investment advantage to a home purchase, then, is practically unbeatable, especially when you look at it in terms of the tax advantages already discussed.

Why You Needn't Worry About High Interest Rates

Most people have little trouble understanding the extremely advantageous position of equity ownership. What they do have trouble with is imagining that they can afford the current high interest rates on mortgage loans.

First of all, what those people really are saying when they bemoan the interest rates is not that the rates are too high but that the monthly carrying charges are unacceptable for their present budgets. But the market is full of opportunities, some of which have already been examined,

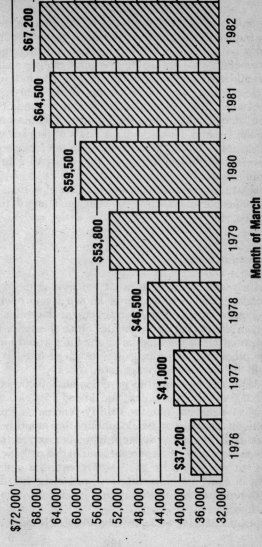

Chart 1, Median Sales Prices of Existing Single-Family Homes in March 1976 - 1982 March, 1976 - 1982

Source; National Association of Realtors.

121

and a bit of creative thinking can be useful here, for there are a number of ways to attack the problem.

One of these ways is *not* to wait until mortgage rates fall to 8 percent as many people are. These are the people who have been left pretty much shell-shocked by the astounding changes in the economic climate that the past decade has seen. They are the people who haven't learned the lesson in Chapter 1 of this book—that in order to survive and thrive in the 1980s and beyond, they must start thinking differently. But because of permanent changes in the banking industry, it's a safe bet that we will never again see 8 percent interest rates on mortgages, unless, of course, we find ourselves in the midst of a full-fledged depression.

That said, there are a good number of options available to prospective homeowners who can't afford those high interest rates.

Seller Financing

First and foremost is what we now refer to as *seller financing* and what used to be known as a *purchase money mortgage*. In this type of arrangement the seller gives the buyer a mortgage on the home. Since the seller would do this to attract a sale that he or she feels would be impossible otherwise, the mortgage rate given often is substantially below bank mortgage rates.

Thus, if you wanted to purchase an $80,000 home with $15,000 as a down payment, you'd need a $65,000 mortgage. The 14½ percent rate on a thirty-year mortgage that the bank might offer you would amount to a monthly expenditure of $771. But a seller might offer you a thirty-year payout mortgage at 11 percent, and in this case the monthly cost to you would be $620—representing a monthly savings of $150, which could very well make the difference between your ability to buy that house and your inability to do so.

Seller financing at below-market rates is quite common,

and as a buyer you should press hard for the most advantageous terms possible.

Buy-downs

Another common vehicle for bringing mortgage rates down is a *buy-down*, and it is quite often found in cases where new condominiums are for sale. In this instance, a builder who is developing a property will make arrangements with a bank to reduce your mortgage interest rate for a specified number of years, usually three or five, after which the normal rates reappear. For example, if a builder is selling you a $90,000 home when interest rates are 15 percent, your monthly cost on a $70,000 mortgage (we're assuming you have the $20,000 down payment) is $886. That builder, however, would be able to sell many more condo units if he could guarantee buyers an up-front mortgage reduction to 11 percent, which would bring down the monthly payment to $668. That would be a savings of more than $200 a month.

Obviously, getting the bank to reduce the mortgage interest for three years is going to cost the builder something. In this case, the cost to the builder for a three-year reduction from 15 to 11 percent is approximately $6,700.

This buy-down type of mortgage is a commonly used marketing tool in reducing mortgage rates for the first three to five years of home ownership. Of course, you involve yourself in this kind of arrangement with the hope that your income will increase in the years to come and that you will be able to afford the higher rates in the future.

Remember that if the seller, who is the builder in this case, is spending a good deal of money to reduce the cost of your mortgage, he will probably be just as willing to reduce the price of the condominium by a comparable amount if you decide to obtain a conventional bank mortgage. Bear in mind that people's needs often dictate a certain flexibility, and that most things, in such cases, are negotiable.

Cash Deals

In addition to seller financing and buy-downs, there is a third way in which you can arrive at more comfortable interest rates, and this involves obtaining a discount in the selling price by offering cash.[3] This type of sale has been common in a number of industries for years and is now becoming common in the real-estate market, especially where condominiums are concerned. It works like this: These days, the market being what it is, most sellers wind up getting involved in seller financing. But by getting the buyers to pay cash, the need for their involvement is eliminated.

For example, a recent home for sale in the Northeast was offered at $79,000 with the seller giving a mortgage at below-market rates. However, the seller made it clear that the price would be reduced to $70,000 for an all-cash sale or if the buyer could make his own mortgage arrangements. In other words, he was offering an 11.4 percent cash discount.

The difficulty with this arrangement is, of course, having the necessary cash. Thus this kind of deal becomes possible most often in a case where the purchasers have just sold a previous residence for more money than the price of the new home. Typically, this would be a retired couple who has decided on a smaller dwelling (such as a condominium) than the one they had previously.

Note that I am not wholeheartedly advocating paying cash for a home, for there are many opportunities available today that could possibly prove more lucrative to the investor with such resources. But if you have the resources and the desire, make sure you get a commensu-

---

[3]As opposed to mortgage financing or any of the other methods discussed here that would reduce the price of the house.

rate discount for the advantage you're offering the seller, and be sure to negotiate carefully.

Why You Needn't Worry About Large Down Payments

So you're convinced that home equity is something you need, and you're even convinced that with a bit of creative financing you can manage those monthly payments. However, the $60,000 mortgage you're getting still leaves $20,000 outstanding against the $80,000 home you've chosen. But you have only $5,000. Is there hope for you? By all means. In fact, there are a number of things you can do.

Second Mortgages

The first way to reduce that down payment would be to get the seller to give you a *second mortgage*. A second mortgage is exactly what it sounds like: a lien on your home in addition to the first mortgage. Typically, a seller-financed second mortgage is short-term—for five years or less—and represents 20 percent of the price of the house. The interest rate, in 1983, would often be below 12 percent.

In the example cited above, the seller would give you a $15,000 second mortgage and five years in which to pay it off. This would reduce the down payment to the $5,000 you have in the following way:

Price of home	$80,000
First mortgage	60,000
Down payment before second mortgage	$20,000
Second mortgage	15,000
Actual down payment	$ 5,000

Why would the seller do that? For two simple reasons: (1) He wants to sell the house and (2) he wants to get top dollar for it.

Of course, a second mortgage would mean that you'd have additional monthly responsibilities, so you must carefully weigh the economic factors and be sure you can handle those payments before you enter into this type of arrangement.

This approach to reducing down payments is very common today, especially among young, two-career couples who have not been able to put much money aside but who have good current income.

Leasing with an Option to Buy

Another way to minimize a down payment is to lease, or rent, a home with an option to buy it. In this type of arrangement, the leasing period usually lasts from one to two years. This practice is not as common as the one mentioned above but is a definite possibility for you nonetheless.

The buyer in this arrangement has two very clear advantages. In the first place, it would give you a chance to evaluate the home, the neighborhood, the community, etc., without committing yourself. The second advantage is that the option to buy would stipulate the selling price of the house at the outset of the lease. This becomes extremely important since the size of the mortgage you would get would be based on the value of the home when you were ready to buy it, which would most likely be higher than the selling price formerly agreed upon. The following illustration may help you to see this more clearly.

Note that since mortgages generally are 78 percent of the *value of the house at the time it is sold*, the mortgage in this particular example would be higher, thus reducing the down payment.

Of course, in this situation, you would have spent money on the rent you would have been paying for the one or two years you leased the house, but chances are, you would have been making monthly payments to live some-

Table 1.
Reduction of Down Payment by Leasing with an Option to Buy

Without Leasing		With Leasing	
Price of home	$90,000	Price of home (established in lease)	$90,000
Mortgage (78% of price of home)	70,200	Appraised value at time of sale	100,000
		Mortgage (78% of appraised value)	78,000
Down payment	$19,800	Down payment	$12,000

where anyway. So if current income is less of a problem for you than coming up with a large chunk of money, leasing with an option to buy is something you should look into.

Using a Buy-down to Reduce a Down Payment

Another method you can explore would be using the buy-down method discussed earlier in this chapter to reduce not the monthly mortgage payments, but the down payment (see pages 123–124). That is, instead of reducing your interest rate or mortgage, an arrangement that could cost the seller, say, $6,000, the seller or builder simply reduces the total cost of the home by $6,000.

Buying a Home at Below-Market Value

Once you've established that you can afford monthly payments *and* a down payment, your creativity need not end, for it would be wise, when house-hunting, to try to obtain your home at a below-market price—that is, a home that because of some special situation is priced below what it might normally cost. There are a number of reasons why a house might be underpriced.

One might be that the owner is selling the house himself. Such sellers have little access to market studies, and as a result, their asking prices are often off the mark. Some, of course, overestimate their properties, but occasionally they underprice, and they do this often enough to make it worth your while to follow up for-sale-by-owner ads every chance you get. Check for this as you go through newspaper ads.

Bear in mind, too, that these sellers save quite a bit of money by avoiding broker commissions, so they may be in a position to accept a lower offer more readily.

Out-of-town owners are another breed of sellers who often underprice homes. There's a good chance that absentee owners may simply not be aware of current market values, and you may be able to get away with below-market offers. Also, these owners may feel more pressed to sell. To find such owners, look for out-of-town phone numbers in local ads.

When searching for a home to buy, don't overlook houses and condominiums that are for rent. Once in a while you'll come across a situation where a house is being rented because the owner was unable to sell it. He may not really want the responsibilities of being a landlord, or he may really need the cash you can offer. In any case, don't be shy about making an offer on such a property. It's likely that you can even buy such a home for just a little more than the mortgage you might get.

Mortgages, Mortgages, Mortgages

The first thing you must understand about shopping for a mortgage is that the days when all banks offered the same terms are long gone. In fact, if you went to two different banks, it's likely you'd get at least five different sets of terms representing several different types of mortgages. The lesson here is that you really must do some legwork to find the mortgage and terms that meet your needs and economic abilities.

The traditional twenty-five- or thirty-year fixed interest and payment mortgage is not dead, but it no longer is the only type available. In this chapter we will discuss just a few of the mortgage options available today. Note carefully that these represent only some of the variations on a basic theme.

The Fixed-Rate Long-Term Mortgage

As I tell my clients, the fixed-rate long-term mortgage is the best type around and should be chosen over all others when it is made available to you. I say this for a number of reasons.

First of all, you know up front exactly what your payments will be over the next twenty-five or thirty years. The beauty of it is that your interest rates are fixed, but your options are kept open, for if interest rates go down, you can refinance or repay the mortgage; if you do this after one year from the date on which the mortgage was obtained, there usually is no prepayment penalty.

It is generally advantageous to get a new mortgage if interest rates drop at least 1½ to 2 percent lower than the terms you have. (Otherwise the cost of refinancing the mortgage would not stack up profitably against the lower terms.) Refinancing, however, is done at *your option*. If interest rates rise (which, of course, they may), you still have your fixed rate.

The Adjustable-Rate Mortgage (ARM)

The adjustable-rate mortgage has the disadvantage of interest rates that change periodically (usually each year, but sometimes more often) to reflect current market interest rates. Your disadvantage is the reason that most banks favor this type of mortgage: They do not want to get stuck again with low interest rates in an inflationary environment. The transitory advantage to these, however—or the sales pitch, if you will—is that these mortgages generally start out with an interest rate that is lower than that of the fixed-rate mortgage. Thus, if you feel that you would only be able to afford your property if first-year payments could be eased up, you're liable to go for this type. Of course, if you're somehow convinced that interest rates will drop in the future, you would view this type of mortgage as advantageous.

The Renegotiable, or Rollover, Mortgage

This mortgage, which first appeared on the West Coast in the 1970s, is similar to the adjustable rate mortgage. In this case you have a mortgage with a twenty-five- or thirty-year payment schedule. But every five years, and sometimes sooner, the mortgage is renegotiated at the current mortgage rate. The fact that the interest rate is fixed for the first five years gives this type of mortgage an advantage over the adjustable-rate mortgage where the rate can change annually, but there is a danger here.

Suppose you purchased a home in January 1977 with a $40,000 five-year rollover mortgage at 8 percent. At the time, you could have gotten a 9½ percent thirty-year fixed rate mortgage but decided against that since you were convinced that interest rates would probably fall very shortly. Also, the lower monthly payments on your 8 percent mortgage took some of the fear out of home ownership. Your mortgage payments were only $294 a month, but since you had to add to that several hundred dollars' worth of utility, maintenance, and tax costs a month, you figured your income could just about support the home you had chosen.

But four and a half years later, January 1982 was fast approaching, and you got a letter from your bank advising you that the new mortgage rate for the next five years had doubled—to 16 percent—and that those monthly payments were about to shoot up to $640. Of course, you could protest, but it wouldn't do you much good. The fact is that the mortgage loan would be due in January 1982 if you did not agree to the new payment schedule.

The point here is that you never really know how high interest rates may go (think the unthinkable!), so try to keep your options open, even if that privilege winds up costing you a bit of money. The lesson is important; bear it in mind.

The Growing-Equity Mortgage (GEM)

The growing-equity mortgage is a fairly new hybrid that is currently being advanced by some institutions. In this type of arrangement, the home purchaser gets a fixed-interest mortgage that is usually 1 percent less than the traditional thirty-year fixed-rate mortgage. To receive that 1 percent advantage, the purchaser agrees to increase the mortgage payments by 4 percent annually, with the extra payments used to reduce the principal of the loan. What happens is that the mortgage gets paid off in less than fifteen years, as opposed to the traditional thirty. The advantage to the bank, of course, is that you use their money for a much shorter period, and they're willing to charge you a lower interest rate in return. The disadvantage to you, of course, is the high monthly payment, which gets higher each year.

Chart 2 compares the monthly payments between growing-equity and fixed-rate mortgages. For purposes of comparison, we assume that both mortgages are based on a 15⅛ percent $80,000 principal balance mortgage over a twenty-five-year period. You can see that for the first year monthly payments are the same, at $1,000, and they stay at that level for twenty-five years with the fixed-rate mortgage. But for the growing-equity mortgage, the monthly payment rises to a little over $1,200 by the sixth year, and

131

Chart 2. Comparison of Monthly Payments Between Growing-Equity and Fixed-Rate Mortgages

Both are based on 15⅛ percent $80,000 principal balance mortgage using a 25 - year amortization schedule.

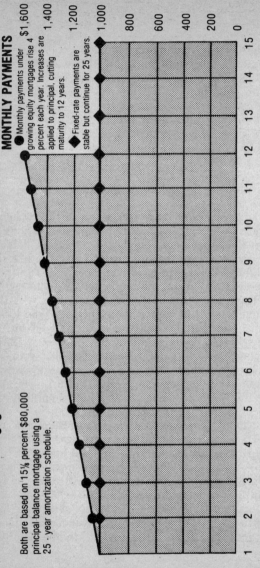

MONTHLY PAYMENTS

● Monthly payments under growing equity mortgages rise 4 percent each year. Increases are applied to principal, cutting maturity to 12 years.

◆ Fixed-rate payments are stable but continue for 25 years.

Year of Mortgage   In the final year, there are 11 monthly payments of $1,589.37 and a final installment of $1,241.23.

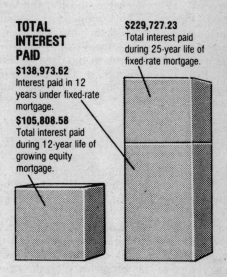

TOTAL INTEREST PAID

$138,973.62
Interest paid in 12 years under fixed-rate mortgage.

$105,808.58
Total interest paid during 12-year life of growing equity mortgage.

$229,727.23
Total interest paid during 25-year life of fixed-rate mortgage.

Source: Federal National Mortgage Association.

by the twelfth and final year, it is up to $1,600, at which time the mortgage is paid off.

The chart further shows that the total interest paid on the GEM loan is substantially lower than that of the fixed-rate mortgage. The GEM interest is $105,808, while the fixed-rate total interest paid is more than double that, $229,727. Of course, this is reasonable, considering that with the GEM you held the money only twelve years as opposed to twenty-five.

For some people, the GEM might be advantageous due to the lower interest charge and the shorter time period involved. But again, I recommend that unless there are extenuating circumstances in your situation, you should try your best to obtain a fixed-rate twenty-five- or thirty-year mortgage. It puts you in the driver's seat and affords you the luxury of open options. This latter point should be your guide in choosing among the real-estate opportunities available to you.

How Much of a House Can You Afford?

When you shop for a mortgage, the major question that the bank will ask—and the one that should be uppermost in your mind as well—is, How large a mortgage can you afford?

Generally, the bank will try to determine whether you have both the ability and desire to pay off a mortgage. In determining this, a bank officer will look at five general factors: (1) income; (2) job security; (3) the size of the down payment you have on hand; (4) credit references; and (5) assets.

Note that your past credit references will be an important consideration, so paying your bills on time should be a priority for you if you ever plan to take out a mortgage. Furthermore, most bankers will agree that the higher down payment you have, the more likely you will be to pay off your mortgage.

Once a bank has decided to give you a mortgage, the

size of it becomes the next major question. Although there are no set rules for determining this, there are some guidelines that can be followed. Some banks adhere to certain ratios loosely. Others regard them as though they were etched in stone. The general formula these days is that your monthly mortgage payment—including principal, interest, real-estate taxes, and homeowner's insurance—should not exceed 28 percent of your monthly verifiable gross income. Thus, for a $60,000, thirty-year, 14 percent fixed-rate mortgage in which your monthly payments would be $711 in addition to another $200 a month for taxes and insurance—bringing that monthly obligation to $911—your monthly income would have to be around $3,250, or approximately $39,000 annually. Of course, the ratio would be examined in light of the other issues mentioned—the stability of your income, the size of the down payment, credit history, etc.

If you strike out the first time you apply for a mortgage, it pays to keep trying, for each bank has different criteria, and the fact is that of all mortgage applicants, 85 percent do wind up with one, even if it isn't exactly the one they had in mind.[4]

Of course, the bank's opinion of what you can afford may differ from your own view of the matter; remember that the bank will, of course, take a most conservative stance on the subject. Realistically, I feel that most people can afford a home whose total expenses—including mortgage, taxes, insurance, utilities, etc.—represent one third of their entire gross income. This situation will definitely involve a good bit of sacrifice and belt-tightening all around, but again, given the advantages of home ownership, the effort is well worth it. And it *can* be done.

---

[4]"What Mortgage Officers Look for in a Borrower," *The New York Times*, September 12, 1982.

Real Estate as an Investment

When we speak of real estate as an investment, we mean real estate that you purchase as other than your own residence. Although this investment is not specifically recommended in Chapter 3, some members of Group B, for whom the purchase of a home was recommended, may be interested in the information that follows if, for example, they are already homeowners but have a chance to buy an especially attractive piece of property at an opportune price. Be advised, however, that the information given here does not by any means constitute all you need to know about being a landlord. You will want to research this subject thoroughly, if it applies to you, by examining some comprehensive texts on the subject. Nevertheless, the points are noteworthy in relation to the previous discussion.

The chances are that for the longest time you've been hearing people say that real estate is a good investment. They claim that you can enjoy good income from the property and yet show on paper (for the IRS, that is) that you've made little or no *taxable* income. Perhaps that has sounded very confusing to you, but everyone says it's so—and even legal.

They're right, and the points that follow should demystify some of the factors that make real estate unique as both an investment and as a tax shelter.

First and foremost, you should know that there is something called *depreciation*. In theory, this simply means that your assets are subject to wear and tear over the course of time, so as they continue to exist, they lessen in value. The simplest example of this, and one you might be familiar with, would be an automobile. Suppose you bought one for $10,000. After two years it's probably worth $6,000 or even less. That represents a $4,000 reduction in value due to depreciation.

As far as real estate is concerned, land cannot be depreciated, only buildings, and only income-producing buildings at that; you can't claim depreciation on your residence. What's more, as you'll see, you can enjoy beautiful depreciation privileges even though your asset actually may have appreciated in value. The best part, of course, is that depreciation is considered an expense item by the IRS and is accordingly deductible.

When you schedule the depreciation of your real estate, you can choose a *recovery period* of, say, fifteen years, which means that you can depreciate your building by 6.67 percent each year for fifteen years. Thus, for a $100,000 building, you can claim $6,670 a year as an expense and call it depreciation. So if your income from the building happened to be $6,670 for the year, you would claim zero profits.

Things got a lot better for real-estate investors in 1981, for that is when the law changed the shortest recovery period on real estate to fifteen years (before that, the shortest recovery period was thirty years[5]) and also allowed something called *accelerated depreciation*, which means that you could claim more depreciation value over the first few years and less over the following years. The following should help you to understand the beauty of accelerated depreciation. We assume that you purchased a $130,000 property ($100,000 for the building and $30,000 for the land) and seek to depreciate it over a fifteen-year recovery period. You can claim depreciation on that property according to the following schedule:

Note that only the building portion of your investment is entitled to depreciation value. This schedule has enabled you to depreciate the value of the building over 20 percent in two years and almost 40 percent in four years.

Remember that depreciation is not an out-of-pocket expense, but only a bookkeeping expense; it helps to shelter your income, or reduce taxes. Without the advantageous depreciation laws, however, the real-estate market would be a lot less favorable than it is in its current state.

There is a slight catch to using accelerated depreciation,

---

[5]Of course, the best advantage to you as a taxpayer is to choose the shortest recovery period available.

Year	Amount of Depreciation Claimed
1st	$ 12,000
2nd	10,000
3rd	9,000
4th	8,000
5th	7,000
6th	6,000
7th	6,000
8th	6,000
9th	6,000
10th	5,000
11th	5,000
12th	5,000
13th	5,000
14th	5,000
15th	5,000
Total depreciation	$100,000

and it's called *recapture rules*. If you sell your building at a profit, any excess depreciation you have claimed (that is, any depreciation greater than the depreciation you would have been entitled to at a normal rate) is "recaptured" by the government, meaning that you must pay tax on the excess depreciation at the ordinary income-tax rate. Still, you'll be happy to do so in that event, since you will at least have been able to defer those taxes for the years you held ownership. Any way you look at it, accelerated depreciation is a good deal.

Remember also that profits made from the sale of an asset held for more than one year are considered capital gains and are thus taxed at a more advantageous rate. The capital gains rate is such that 60 percent of the profit is tax-free and 40 percent is taxed at your ordinary income-tax rate. Thus, real-estate investors are major beneficiaries of capital-gains tax laws.

A Word of Caution About Real Estate as an Investment

Buying real estate for income and profit is not an easy or straightforward proposition, and as I've said earlier, you'd want to research the area thoroughly before making a move in this direction. If you have many doubts, you're probably better off dropping the idea, for numerous responsibilities and costs are involved in landlording.

If you do decide to take the step, make sure you do a very thorough analysis of the area in which you're considering buying property. A man wiser than I once listed the three most important considerations in real estate as (1) location; (2) location; and (3) location. That may be something of an exaggeration, but bear in mind that generally most real estate is not movable and that surrounding areas are one of the key variables in the rising or falling value of your property. Although I am a very strong advocate of buying in the best locations for investment purposes, remember that often you can overpay for these and that a comparable piece of property in a less favorable location and, therefore, priced lower may often prove to be a better investment.

In all aspects of the real-estate purchases you make, remember that practically anything can be a good investment at the right price.

9

Gold

Of all the investments discussed in this book, gold probably is the riskiest. Nevertheless, it is included here since it has proven itself to be an excellent inflation hedge when viewed as a long-term investment. Had you purchased a gold Krugerrand for $103 in July 1975, you would have enjoyed a 700 percent profit in January 1980, when gold soared to an astounding $875 an ounce. Although it is improbable that this situation will repeat itself, profits still are likely to be had in the gold market, and these will be described here.

Although much of what we are about to say about gold is true of silver as well, I have recommended the former and not the latter simply because gold has, without question, proven itself as one of *the* best hedges against inflation and economic instability. (This is not true of silver, nor of any other precious metal or gem.) In addition, gold is universally recognized as a storer of value. The following short history of gold should give you some understanding of how gold earned its reputation.

Ever since biblical times, gold has been held in high esteem for its rarity, its beauty, and its use as currency. In fact, until modern times, the wealth of nations was measured by their gold holdings.

Prior to 1933, the price of an ounce of gold was fixed, by the government, at $21. That is, the government guaranteed that they would buy or sell gold at that price, give or take minor commissions.

During this pre-1933 period, gold coins and gold certificates circulated freely. A $5 or $10 gold piece was a common gift for a child's birthday. This was the time when gold was the total monetary standard; you could exchange paper money for gold.

During the Great Depression, this situation changed dramatically. First of all, Congress forbade the holding of gold bullion—all gold that was not in the form of jewelry, dental fillings, or rare coins. They did this because they felt that as the Depression progressed, more and more people would convert their dollars to gold, thus reducing the government's stockpile and depressing the value of the dollar. All citizens were ordered to turn in their gold coins and certificates. Furthermore, in 1933 the government raised the price of gold from $21 to $35 an ounce.

Although all the economic and political reasons for these moves are beyond the scope of this book, suffice it to say that the government felt these techniques would help to overcome the Depression and to further subsequent economic growth. The ban on gold, which would last for over forty years, put greater wealth in the hands of Uncle Sam.

As we have mentioned, the United States government established the official price of gold at $35 an ounce in 1933, and this price remained until the U.S. dollar was devaluated in 1972, bringing the gold price up to $38 an ounce, and again in 1973, at which time gold rose to $42.22 an ounce. (As the price of gold rises, the value of the dollar, which is relative to the value of gold, is reduced.) But starting in 1968, international economic pressures caused the creation of an independent pricing tier for open-market gold transactions, and the price began to move upward. This was only logical, since the price had been kept artificially low for over thirty-five years.

In 1973 the official government gold pricing system was completely abandoned, and at the start of 1975, Americans were allowed to own gold bullion for the first time since 1933. The open, broadscale trading in gold, the continuing inflationary pressures, and the new participants in the gold market—U.S. citizens—stimulated the steep price rise to $200 an ounce on the first day of 1975.

Unfortunately for the gold speculators, however, during the following months most Americans did not stampede to their banks, brokers, and coin dealers, probably because they did not have, as the Europeans did, the tradition of gold as a hedge against political turmoil. Gold simply had not been a reality to most Americans within their lifetimes. Thus there wasn't nearly the demand for gold that the speculators had anticipated, and, as often happens with a "sure thing," the price of gold fell to a paltry $103 an ounce by July of that year.

For some, however, this was an opportunity in disguise; by January 1980, the price of gold tapped out at $875 an ounce.

Of course, the price had not gone straight up; it hit a few peaks and valleys on its way from $103 to $875 an ounce, and these are illustrated in Chart 1. The sharp rise and fall of the price of gold for the years shown should tell you something else: Gold prices—and gold investments—are tricky business.

Note that in mid-1979 the price of gold was in the $250-an-ounce range. Just six months later, by January 1980, it had leaped to $875, constituting a rise of over 300 percent in less than a year. But that pendulum can swing in both directions, for by June 1982, gold had dropped to $297 an ounce—a 66 percent drop.

Thus, had you invested $5,000 in gold in January 1980, you would have wound up with only $1,700 by the time gold hit $297 in June 1982. However, had you purchased it in June 1982, you would have had a handsome sum of

$8,000 just three months later, in September 1982, when gold had approached $500 an ounce.

But as with all other investment areas, past performance cannot be used to predict the future accurately. Furthermore, the performance that Chart 1 illustrates represents statistics only. How those gold prices came to rise and fall as they did can be understood only by examining the forces that affect gold prices and commodities and financial securities in general.

What Affects Gold Prices?

Basically, three general forces affect gold prices: supply and demand; inflation; and political instability. Although they may be examined separately, it is important to understand that they work together to produce market changes and that these resulting changes cannot always be traced to one particular source. Moreover, these three factors are obviously dependent on others: Inflation often is affected by oil prices, which in turn can affect political instability, and so on. The important thing to remember is that predictability in any one of these areas does not necessarily allow one to predict what the price of gold will be in, say, two months.

Supply and Demand

Supply and demand is a fundamental element in understanding any commodity. Simply put, when demand rises faster than supply, prices go up. Conversely, when a surplus in any commodity exists, demand—and prices—go down.

Gold always has been in limited supply because it is difficult to locate and mine in quantity. One source estimates that throughout history only eighty-eight thousand

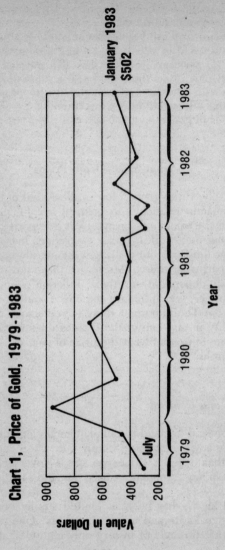

Chart 1, Price of Gold, 1979-1983

January 1983
$502

tons of gold have been mined—a quantity that would fit into a cube measuring eighteen yards on each side.[1]

Annual world mining of gold amounts to about fourteen hundred tons, for which the leading producers are: South Africa (55 percent), the U.S.S.R. (23 percent), Canada (4 percent), and the United States (2 percent). After peaking in the mid-1960s, non-Communist-world production was reduced 25 percent by the beginning of the 1980s due to the difficulty of finding and the expense of extracting gold from mines. In fact, in South Africa, mining companies must process three to five tons of earth for every one ounce of pure gold that is turned up. This factor helped South African gold production to decline from eleven hundred tons annually in 1970 to less than eight hundred tons by the early 1980s. It is estimated that by the end of this century it will fall to approximately four hundred tons a year.[2]

What also tends to affect the supply of gold is the sale of hoards of it by, for instance, Middle East interests or by the Soviet Union, which sells gold when it finds itself in need of world currency for grain purchases. It must be remembered that most world events have a direct or indirect effect on the price of gold.

The demand for gold comes traditionally from three basic sources: for jewelry; for industry; and for investments. Until recently jewelry accounted for about 70 percent of the demand, but increased prices, especially during the 1979–80 period, caused the annual use of gold for jewelry to drop from eleven hundred tons to approximately seven hundred to eight hundred tons, which is a decrease of about a third.

Industrial uses of gold account for approximately 10 percent of its total demand. The abilities of gold to reflect heat, resist corrosion, and conduct electricity have given it special importance within the electronics and aerospace industries. Also, gold's special properties have made it quite useful in dentistry.

---

[1]Deak and Perera, 630 Fifth Avenue, New York, NY 10111.
[2]Deak and Perera, 630 Fifth Avenue, New York, NY 10111.

Gold has traditionally been an excellent storer of value and thus has recognized value throughout the world. Because of its scarcity and its use as a worldwide medium of exchange, gold actually has increased in real value while paper currencies have fluctuated dramatically as a function of governmental, economic, and social changes.

While the demand for gold jewelry has been reduced due to the rise in the price of gold, the demand for gold in bar or coin form has risen to the extent that it now accounts for about 50 percent of current gold demand. Also, central banks all over the world are turning increasingly to gold to protect national reserves from inflation, to enhance their international trade, and to help strengthen their economies.

Inflation

One thing we do know about gold is that at least for the past decade it has proved to be a very good hedge against inflation. From Table 1 we can see that for the past five- and ten-year periods, gold's rate of return was 17.3 percent and 18.6 percent, respectively. These increases were substantially higher than the rate of inflation, which was 9.6 percent and 8.6 percent, respectively, for those periods.

Table 1.
Various Rates of Return for Five- and Ten-Year Periods

	Compounded Annual Returns	
	For 5-Year Period Ending June 1, 1982	For 10-Year Period Ending June 1, 1982
Consumer Price Index	9.6%	8.6%
Gold	17.3%	18.6%
Silver	5.5%	13.6%
Stocks	7.7%	3.9%
Bonds	0.6%	3.6%
Housing	10.0%	9.9%

Source: Salomon Brothers, Inc., 55 Water Street, New York, NY 10001.

Thus, since we can conclude that inflation has been a major factor in the performance of gold over long periods, and since it seems likely from my point of view that inflation will go up over the next several years, it would seem to make sense that gold prices would benefit from the rise.

But predictions cannot be based on the simple assumption that if inflation goes up, gold prices will automatically follow, for dealers in all marketable commodities, including those of gold, stocks, bonds, and even pork bellies, try to anticipate the future. Thus, in the gold market, the price may fall just at the time inflation is highest because speculators are betting that inflation will then fall and gold will do likewise. So they sell their gold, creating a greater supply in the marketplace and lower prices. This is a classic illustration of just how hazardous such predictions can be.

Do interest rates have an effect on the price of gold? The answer is a definite yes. In fact, one of the probable reasons that the price of gold fell from the $850 level in early 1980 to the $300 level two years later is that interest rates generally were at an historically high level during that period. Holding gold during high-interest periods is a rather unattractive investment since gold does not pay dividends, as other investments do. Why, for instance, would someone invest in gold at a time when U.S. treasury bills are guaranteeing a 15 percent annual return? Thus, during that 1980–82 period, many investors sold their gold in favor of other investment vehicles, thereby causing the price of gold to drop.

Bear in mind that this situation also can occur as investors *anticipate* high interest rates; in fact, it is the anticipation component that makes the market so interesting—and so awesome.

It is interesting to note that higher inflation rates tend to increase the price of gold, while higher interest rates tend to bring it down. But high interest rates usually go hand in hand with high inflation rates. How does that figure? The answer is that sometimes the inflation rate is more dominant in dictating gold prices, while at other times it's interest rates. This brings us back to the point made earlier: Predictability in any one of three factors that affect gold does not necessarily tell us anything definite about gold prices.

Political Instability

Generally speaking, when the world is at war or when revolutions and political upheaval take place, many investors make a dash for gold, since it is the one security that has held up against currency devaluations, government changes, and revolution. Thus, as more and more countries experience unstable economies and governments (two factors that often go hand in hand), gold becomes a more alluring investment. In fact, during times of severe economic or political upheaval, this instability becomes by far the most dominant factor affecting the price of gold. During such times, investors are less interested in possible returns than they are in simply maintaining the value of their money.

A recent example is the case of the Mexican peso. In early 1982 the peso was worth about $.04, or 25 pesos to the dollar, as it is put. Gold was then about $400 an ounce, and a Mexican could have bought one ounce of gold for 10,000 pesos. That would have been an astute move, for by January 1983, the peso had dropped to $0.0067, or 150 to the dollar, constituting a decrease in the value of the peso of over 80 percent. Assuming, for the purpose of our example, that gold stayed at $400 an ounce,[3] that Mexican investor would have maintained his purchasing power in terms of dollars, for his one ounce of gold, for which he paid 10,000 pesos, would be worth 60,000 pesos.

During the past decade, the most dominant factor affecting the price of gold has been the phenomenal rise in the price of oil, which obviously comes under the heading of

---

[3]It didn't. By this time it was selling for $480 an ounce.

political and economic instability. In 1972 crude oil sold for $2.00 to $3.00 a barrel; by late 1982 the price had gone up to $34 a barrel, representing a 1,300 percent increase. That equals about a 29 percent annual compound rate of return and is more than double the inflation rate for that decade. Gold, of course, followed a similar pattern during that decade, going from approximately $35 to $40 an ounce in 1972 to over $500 an ounce by 1982.

Thus we've seen how three major factors—supply and demand, inflation, and political instability—affect gold prices and that these are so closely tied to interest rates and oil prices that they become inseparable. It is important to bear in mind, however, that during the 1980s new factors that affect the price of gold may emerge.

At the time of this writing, gold prices are about $400 to $430 an ounce. Basing my predictions on future inflation and interest rate trends, I would say that the price will soon drop to around $325 and then reemerge to surpass the $500-an-ounce level in early 1984. Fluctuations between $300 and $500 probably will occur several times before the price of gold goes far beyond $500 in the mid-1980s.

How to Invest in Gold

The most popular and easiest way for the individual investor to buy gold is to purchase coins that have *no numismatic value*—that is, they are valuable only for the gold they contain and not for their value as collectible coins. Those coins having no numismatic value are frequently called *bullion* coins. The two best types to have are the Canadian Maple Leaf and the South African Krugerrand. The weight and purity of these coins are commonly accepted, which is important, for unlike gold bars and some other coins, there is no need to have them assayed for gold purity upon purchase or resale. Furthermore, their value can be easily determined according to the daily price of gold, which is published in financial and some general newspapers.

Table 2 shows the price on a given day of the three most common bullion coins and their *wholesale premium value above their gold content.* That is their value as coins above their value as gold, which in the cases shown is fairly low, at about 3 percent each. Each of these coins weighs approximately one ounce. Note that *wholesale* premium values are shown; dealers mark these prices up at rates that may vary from 3% to 10%. Thus, when you shop around for gold purchases, look for the dealer whose mark-ups are the lowest. Furthermore, try to buy from the most reputable dealer available, since there have been reports of counterfeit bullion gold coins. To find the best dealer, ask your bank for a good reference or simply try to deal with the largest one in your area.

The best coins to purchase are those of one-ounce weight, which was once standard for both the South African Krugerrand and the Mexican coin. The Krugerrand now

Table 2.
Prices and Wholesale Premium Values of Gold Coins on January 15, 1983

| | Price of Coin | Premium Above Value of Gold Contained in Coin | |
		Per Coin	As Percent of Gold Value
South African Krugerrand	$504.00	$15.50	3.17
Canadian Maple Leaf	503.00	14.50	2.97
1-ounce Mexican coin	503.50	15.00	3.07

Note: The price of gold on January 15, 1983, was $488.50 an ounce.
Source: Barron's, January 17, 1983.

comes in one-half-ounce, one-fourth-ounce, and one-tenth-ounce weights, while the Mexican coin now is available in one-half-ounce and one-quarter-ounce weights. These are not recommended, however, since premium rates on gold coins go up as gold content is reduced, so try to buy the full one-ounce weight, if possible.

The coins shown in Table 2 may be purchased from coin dealers, brokerage houses, and many banks. As we've mentioned, whichever you choose, check out the reputation and reliability of the seller.

When you buy these coins, you will have to pay sales tax on them, unless they are purchased through the mail from another state.

Table 3 shows two reliable firms that sell Krugerrands through the mail. For a small fee, both of these companies will store the coins for you and give you a certificate of storage, and each has an excellent reputation.

Table 3.
Two Reliable Ways to Purchase Krugerrands Through the Mail Without Paying Sales Tax

Company	Minimum Purchase	Premium	Shipping Fee	Storage Fee	Commission
Dreyfus Fund 767 Fifth Avenue New York, NY 10153 For information: (800)645-6561 For purchases: (800)223-7750	10	$19–25 per coin	$30 flat fee	$0.15 per ounce per month	$10 per coin
Deak and Perera 630 Fifth Avenue New York, NY 10111 (800)225-1709	none	about 5% of total purchase	varies	free through the end of the calendar year (including insurance). Thereafter, ½% per year.	2½% on initial purchase; 1% to sell

There are, of course, many ways to invest in gold. The methods mentioned above are most appropriate for readers of this book, but you might be interested in the pros and cons of a few others.

Gold futures are highly risky investments that are made through your stockbroker. The minimum investment is $1,000 on margin (which involves making investments using lots of borrowed funds) per hundred-ounce contract. Delivery on a purchase such as this is rarely taken. It provides leverage as an investment, there are no storage or insurance costs, and commissions run about $65–$70 per contract. But given the size of the investment and the volatility of the market, losses can be great,[4] so I strongly advise that you stay away from this type of purchase.

Stocks involve purchasing stock in gold mining companies. Most of these are located in South Africa and therefore are associated with substantial political and economic unrest. Shares in these companies are sold through the stock market and are traded over the counter. (Most brokerage houses will be happy to send you a list of major gold mining companies on request.) Most gold shares pay substantial dividends, but again, given the turmoil in South Africa and the fact that the prices of the stocks experience more extreme changes than the prices of gold bullion coins, I'd stay away from this risky method of investment.

A more conservative way to invest in the stocks of gold mining companies is through gold mutual funds. These, as all mutual funds, give you diversification and professional management for your money. But remember that you still are at the mercy of the gold mining companies themselves, making this method speculative as well.

Gold certificates are nontransferable statements of gold ownership which allow you to purchase gold without ever taking possession of it. There is no sales tax, but storage and insurance costs must be paid, and there is a 2½

---

[4]Profits also may be significant.

percent sales commission if the certificates are bought through a broker (they usually are). The minimum purchase is $2,500.

Jewelry. It's nice to wear, there's no minimum purchase, and it may pay a premium over the intrinsic value of the gold it contains, but the quality of gold varies so greatly and the gold content is so difficult to assess and therefore keep track of values, that I'd suggest this form be avoided as an investment.

The big problem with gold jewelry is that you purchase it at retail prices and usually sell it at wholesale prices. Since the markup on gold jewelry usually is 100 percent but can go as high as 300 percent, it would not be uncommon for someone to buy a gold bracelet for $1,000 on one day that they could sell for only $500 the following week.[5]

As we've seen in this chapter, gold is potentially a high-return investment. But since it's a volatile one, it has been recommended only for a select group of investors—those who can afford the risk—and even in this instance, you will note, it has not been suggested as a majority asset in any portfolio.

---

[5]A jewelry markup of 200 to 300 percent is not uncommon.

10

Electric Utility Stocks

As you probably noticed when reviewing the recommended portfolios in Chapter 3, I have steered clear of stock investments in specific companies, with mutual fund investments being a close exception. But electric utility stocks are a different story altogether, for they offer one of the most favorable investments for the 1980s, and their ability to do this owes much to government intervention.

In 1981 the United States Congress, with the consent of the President, passed a law called the Economic Recovery Act of 1981.[1] There are numerous provisions to this law, some of which we have already seen at work. One specific part addressed itself to the needs of the utility industry, which was suffering at the time. This provision was known as the Dividend Reinvestment Program (or DRIP, if you will) of the 1981 Tax Act. Its purpose was to induce people to invest in the utility companies; to accomplish that, it provided the following:

A qualified public utility may establish a dividend reinvestment program under which individual shareholders

---

[1] Unfortunately, despite the name, economic recovery did not occur that year, nor in the year that followed.

who want to reinvest dividends in the common stock of the company may do so and then exclude up to $750 from the income shown on an individual tax return and up to $1,500 from a joint return. (Interestingly, married individuals can exclude $1,500 even if only one spouse owns the stock or receives the dividends.)

Instead of receiving cash dividends, electric utility stock investors receive newly issued common stock, and this stock, if held for at least a year, qualifies as a reinvested dividend. If sold before the year is out, the funds received for the sale of the stock are considered ordinary income, and there is no tax advantage.

Once these dividend stocks are held for more than a year, then upon sale, the funds are taxed as capital gains— that is, 60 percent of the income is tax-free while the other 40 percent is taxed at the rate for ordinary income. What you're getting, then, is the advantage of having over half your income on these stocks tax-free. Not bad in these taxing times.

Let's look at an example. Suppose you bought stock in a *nonqualified* electric utility company[2] that offered a $1,500 dividend. That entire dividend would be 100 percent taxable at your normal income-tax rate, which we will suppose is the 35 percent bracket. You would wind up paying $525 in taxes (35 percent of $1,500) on that dividend.

But take the same dividend from a qualified electric utility company and compare the numbers. Only 40 percent of that $1,500 dividend is taxable once you've held it for over a year. That means you pay 35 percent of $600 (40 percent of $1,500), or a total of $210. Thus, because you have invested in a *qualified* utility, you are able to pocket an extra $315.

To sweeten the pot further, many companies provide a discount when purchasing common stock with reinvested dividends. It is this reinvestment program combined with the DRIP provisions described above that make electric

---

[2] Or in a nonutility company.

utility stocks such a favorable investment. It is important to know, however, that DRIP was installed as a temporary measure; unless it is extended, it will expire on December 31, 1985. (Repeal of this provision actually was considered as part of the 1982 tax law but failed to pass.)

Finding the Right Stock

To take the mystery out of finding the right electric utility stock to invest in, I will, later in this chapter, make seven specific recommendations that cater to different investment objectives. But before you choose from that group, it is important to understand all the advantages that make electric utility investing so favorable. These, of course, exist in addition to the tax treatment described above.

One of the factors on which my recommendations are based is a projected annual return over the next five years that averages 15 percent or more. This is based on a projected annual dividend return of about 10 or 11 percent in addition to price appreciation of 4 to 5 percent a year, which is a reasonably conservative estimate and one that bears some discussion.

The government regulators of electric utility companies are conciliatory toward the industry they serve and view rate increases in light of economic realities, as well they should. However, this was not always the case, as the mid- to late 1970s period proves. At that time, electric utility companies were hard pressed to convince government that rate increases (which must, by law, be approved by state public service commissions) were in order. As a result, the industry suffered. The fact that the government has reversed its view on the matter is one of the factors that makes these investments so favorable at present.

Another factor that makes the electric utility industry attractive to investors has to do with conservation of energy.

Since its advent, the need for greater plant construction—and subsequent large-scale financing—has been reduced substantially. This dramatic change has further aided the industry by reducing the need to issue large construction bonds with their high interest rates and high costs. Thus one of the major costs of utilities—financing—has been reduced.

As all other stocks, electric utility stocks are highly sensitive to interest rates, and given the likelihood that interest rates are likely to rise during 1984, it can be assumed that these stocks will suffer somewhat. I would predict, however, that in the long run (meaning over the next two to five years) the performance of those stocks recommended on page 159 will more than compensate for the interest rate factor because their dividends will be raised often during this period. Note that all of the recommendations made in Table 1 are based on the following criteria:

1. A favorable earnings outlook—that is, one in which earnings are estimated to increase greater than 6 percent per annum or an estimated annual total rate of return over the next five years of 15 to 16 percent.

2. A projection of consistent and growing dividends.

3. A favorable state regulatory climate that looks upon rate increases in realistic economic terms.

4. No nuclear involvement or a functioning or completed nuclear program, thus reducing the enormous expenses, possible liabilities, and cost overruns of nuclear plants. This also helps the public image of the company.

5. Strong financial integrity; a good balance between assets and liabilities.

6. Relatively low common dividend payouts—that is, 50 percent or so of earnings paid as dividends.

7. A qualified (by government) dividend reinvestment program (brokers know which companies are qualified).

Note that the terms *growth* and *moderate growth*, as used in the table, are arbitrary ratings. Generally speaking, a growth company may be expected to have increased earnings of 8 to 10 percent a year. A moderate-growth company may be expected to have increased earnings of 5 to 7 percent a year.

The term *current yield* refers to current dividends divided by the market price of the stock. Thus, for a stock selling at $20 a share whose annual dividend is $2.00 a share, the current yield would be $2.00 divided by $20, or 10 percent.

Common stock dividend increases refers to the number of times during the period mentioned that stock dividends were raised. The notation "9 of 10," for instance, would mean that of ten dividend payments, nine constituted raises over the previous dividend payment.

Finally, the column called *dividend growth rates* shows the average annual increase in dividends for the period 1976–81.

As far as the first point in the list is concerned, I recommend less preoccupation with current yields than I do with long-term growth. Of course, though, current yield is a factor. A reasonable current yield would be 8 to 10 percent, for if a dividend has been growing at an average rate of 8 percent a year, it can be expected to double in roughly nine years. Note that all of the seven companies recommended have reasonable current dividend yields of between 8.5 and 10.2 percent. In addition, most are moderate-growth prospects and all except one offer a 5 percent discount on dividend reinvestment.

Remember always that variables and economic factors change rapidly. Once you choose a stock, it is important to stay on top of it by reevaluating future projections often. This can be accomplished by consulting your stockbroker as well as *Standard & Poor's Industry Survey* and *Moody's Industry Survey*, which are available in many libraries. I view the companies I have recommended as your best bets for electric utility stock investments, but past performance does not always resemble future growth, and the

Table 1.
Recommended Electric Utility Stocks

Company	Rating	Discount on Dividend Reinvesting	Price per Share on Jan. 21, 1983	Current Yield	Common Stock Dividend Increases, 1972–81	Dividend Growth Rates, 1976–81
Consolidated Edison	Growth	No	19¾	8.5%	7 times* (1975–81)	13.1%
Texas Utilities	Growth	5%	23¼	8.8%	10 of 10 (1972–81)	7.3%
Southwestern Public	Moderate growth	5%	16½	9.8%	9 of 10 (1972–81)	6.4%
Wisconsin Power and Light	Moderate growth	5%	26¼	8.8%	9 of 11 (1972–82)	5.5%
New England Electric	Moderate growth	5%	33½	9.0%	8 of 10 (1972–81)	8.5%
Public Service of Colorado	Moderate growth	5%	17¼	10.2%	6 of 10 (1972–81)	2.8%
Hawaiian Electric	Moderate growth	5%	32½	9.2%	9 of 10 (1972–81)	8.6%

*In 1974 Consolidated Edison cut its dividends due to economic and political considerations.

159

government provisions that make these investments so attractive can change, so be sure to do your homework consistently. Of course, these purchases should be made through a stockbroker; finding a diligent one will help enormously.

11

For High Rollers Only

The world is awash with get-rich-quick schemes, and unfortunately enough people are willing to take that plunge to keep such "opportunities" constantly available. The fact that you'd be rich today if you had $5.00 for each time the Brooklyn Bridge has been sold is as much a tribute to the salesmanship of many sharp operators as it is to the public craving for instant money.

I am always amazed to hear otherwise sane, conservative, objective individuals talk with great enthusiasm about the relative value of some penny stocks, for instance, whose product they know little about and care not at all. Too many people feel that if they could just make that one important connection with the guy who seems to know it all, they'd make millions. It's true that if you bought enough IBM stock in 1950, you'd be wealthy today. Unfortunately, it is examples such as this that cause people to search constantly for fast money. It's true, also, that such a stock market opportunity may come along again, but you can bet it won't come from someone who makes a concerted effort to sell you the idea. Let's face it: Those in the know—or those who at least think they are—don't really want to share this "inside" information with you.

My advice to those incorrigible souls who feel sure that the next hot tip (cabdrivers are known to have plenty of these; after all, don't they hear everything that goes on?) will make them independently wealthy is to find a better way. If you fall into this group, consider a short trip to Las Vegas or Atlantic City. You may hit the jackpot, you're likely to enjoy your stay, and you'll get a few free drinks on the side. Or you could try any one of the state lotteries; after all, millions of dollars are won in them weekly.

But what do you do if all the flights to Las Vegas and Atlantic City are booked and your state doesn't operate a lottery? More to the point, what do you do if you've got $5,000 that you are *financially and psychologically prepared to lose*? This chapter speaks to your needs.

Be forewarned on a number of points. In the first place, what follows here are not investments but *speculations*. Their successful outcome depends on your having the wherewithall to predict market changes, which, of course, requires you to be fairly comfortable with the workings of the stock and bond markets. Most people do not fit into this category.

In the second place, the funds you use should be those you are in a position to lose without having that loss result in major financial or psychological repercussions. Of course, nobody *likes* to lose, but if the money you're thinking of using is earmarked for mortgage payments, or if a possible loss would affect you strongly, then stay away, by all means. In short, be prepared for the worst possible outcome.

The speculative investments that follow are high-risk, to be sure, and there is no doubt that you *can*, if things go your way, literally double or triple your money within a few months or even a few weeks. Of course, it follows that you can lose your investment in such short order as well.

These investments employ the concept of leverage, which

we have already seen at work in the chapter on real estate. Briefly, leverage allows you to use a small amount of your own money and a lot of someone else's to control a large investment. Thus, if your investment makes money, your profit is accentuated by the fact that you never had to put up all the money to cover it in the first place. Of course, you pay for this privilege: If the investment fails, which these often do, your losses are dramatic, for you are possibly out your total investment commitment.

Speculating in U.S. Government Long-Term Bonds

Let's start out with a short refresher course on bonds, which were discussed in Chapter 6 on U.S. government securities. U.S. government bonds are long-term obligations of the federal government. All bonds pay interest, and they can be sold before maturity. Once issued, the market value of the bond is controlled by interest rate changes. When interest rates rise, the value of the bond goes down; conversely, when interest rates drop, the bond price goes up.

Speculating in the bond market is different from buying bonds because when you purchase them outright, you pay your money and hope for the best. Speculation, on the other hand, means that you try to forecast interest rates and subsequent bond values *before you actually buy the bonds*.

The first thing you need is a crystal ball—or some other method of predicting interest rates. Let's assume that one way or another you have become convinced that interest rates are about to fall. If you're correct and you have $5,000 to spend, substantial rewards will be yours.

You start by using your $5,000 to buy $50,000 worth of bonds on margin. Buying on margin means, in this case, that you put up $5,000, and a broker gives you a $45,000 loan for the rest. Of course, you are charged for this loan at about 1 or 2 percent above the prime rate.

Two actively traded long-term bonds that are commonly used for this sort of speculation are the 10⅜ percent bonds that are scheduled to mature in the year 2012, and the 14 percent bonds that will mature in 2011. The prices of these bonds are published daily in the financial sections of most newspapers.

We'll assume that the price of the bond you've chosen is $1,000, that the yield on the bond is 12 percent, and that you buy fifty of them. If your loan rate is 14 percent, all this means that you have $50,000 worth of bonds on which you're receiving $6,000 interest income (12 percent × $50,000) annually and spending $7,000 (14 percent × $50,000) annually on interest expenses on a margin loan.

Now, suppose you were right and that in a month interest rates on these bonds fall from 12 to 11 percent. Here's what happens. The value of each bond goes up to $1,050, an increase of 5 percent. If you sell all of your bonds now, you will get a total of $52,500 minus that month's share of interest expense, but plus that month's share of your interest income. Here's how the numbers look so far:

Original bond purchase (50 bonds at $1,000, each yielding 12% annually)	$50,000
Value of bonds after 5% increase	52,500
Plus interest income	+500
	53,000
Minus interest expense (on 14% margin loan)	−583
Proceeds	52,417
Cost of original bond purchase	−50,000
Profit before commission	2,417
Minus approximate commission on sale	−250
Net profit	$ 2,167

Thus you've made a profit of $2,167 on a $5,000 investment—or a 43 percent return—in one short month. Now, if you could be as accurate in your predictions every month for a year (and some people do try!), your annual rate of return, assuming all interest is compounded, would be an astronomical 7,300 percent. Put another, more alluring way, your $5,000 investment would be worth over $365,000—by the simple maneuver of calling a 1 percent turn in interest rates each month for one year. Doing it every month, of course, would be extremely difficult; your success in only one month would mean a 43 percent return, which is quite good indeed.

In this example, your interest rate speculation turned out well because the interest rate went down, as you predicted. But what would have happened if you were wrong and rates did not fall to 11 percent but rose instead to 13 percent? You would have lost over 50 percent of your money, and to make matters worse, your broker probably would have asked for additional money down. This is quite common and is known as a *margin call*. Here's what that situation would have looked like:

Original bond purchase (50 bonds at $1,000, each yielding 12% annually)	$50,000
Value of bonds after interest rates rise to 13% and bond price falls to $950	47,500
Plus interest income	+500
	48,000
Less interest expense on margin loan	−583
Net proceeds before commission	47,417
Less cost of original bonds	−50,000
Less before commission	−2,583
Less commissions	−250
Net loss	$ 2,833

You would have lost $2,833 after starting out with $5,000. That comes to a 57 percent loss. Now, just imagine what would have happened if interest rates had gone up not 1 percent but 2 percent!

As you can see, interest rate speculation is not for everyone. Even if you do wind up ahead, bear in mind that the ulcer you may develop in the process may not be worth your profits.

The Option Market

Still no available flights to Las Vegas? Here's another alternative; it's called the option market.

There are two types of options. One is known as *a call*, which means an option to buy a stock at a specified price for a specified period of time. The other type of option is called *a put*, which is an option to sell a stock at a specified price for a specified period of time.

Once again, leverage becomes part of the attraction of this type of speculation; it accentuates your profits—and, unfortunately, your losses.

Let's assume that you're quite sure IBM stock will go up in the next six months and you want to maximize your possible profits. Instead of simply buying the stock, you buy a call option. Suppose the stock is selling for $100 a share and the option to buy the stock at that price (regardless of whether it goes up or down) for the next six months would cost approximately $8.00 a share.[1] The $8.00 is what you pay for the privilege of being able to buy the stock at $100 a share for the next six months. You're actually paying for time. (Note that you never actually own the stock, just the option to purchase it.)

Now let's suppose that within six months the price of IBM stock goes up to $116. The price of your *option* will probably then be worth at least $16, depending on the amount of time left. The more time remaining on the option, the higher the price will be above $16.

So you did it again: The stock went up 16 percent (from $100 to $116 a share), and the value of your option doubled.

---

[1] The price of the option is dictated by supply and demand as well as the price of the stock. The more volatile the stock, the higher the call option percentage premium.

What you've done is double your investment before commissions. Not bad for a beginner.

But what if you were wrong and at the end of six months IBM stock was down to 99¾? The value of your option would be zero, for who'd want to buy a $99.75 stock for $100 a share? What's worse is that had the stock stayed at $100 a share, your option, which would have expired at the end of the six-month period, would still be worthless.

This latter example, in fact, is what usually happens. Yes, the option market can yield highly attractive profits, but the plain truth is that most investors who buy options usually lose their money.

There is another way to play the options game, however, and it works like this: Let's say you don't know which direction the stock market—and one particular stock—are going, but you're sure they're going somewhere, meaning it's a volatile market.[2]

To hedge your bet in the option market, you could buy a put (an option to sell) *and* a call (an option to buy) on the same stock. An example will be useful here.

Suppose that on a given date, the price of American Telephone & Telegraph stock is $70 a share. The six-month call at $75 is about $1.00. That means that during that six-month period, you have a right to buy the stock at $75 a share. Further, the six-month put at $65 is also priced at about $1.00, meaning that during that time you have the right to sell your stock at $65 a share. You feel sure that American Telephone & Telegraph will move significantly one way or another, but you're not sure which way, so you buy both options—a put and call together—which combination is called a *straddle*.

Now let's take several different scenarios. The following set of numbers shows a variety of stock values at the end

---

[2]In fact, I feel quite sure that stock market volatility will be increasing significantly in the near future and throughout the 1980s and that fifty-point moves, both up and down in the Dow Jones Industrial Index, will not be uncommon.

of the six-month period along with the value of the call, the value of the put, and your profit or loss in each case, assuming that you bought ten contracts of puts and ten contracts of calls, both at $1.00 per share for a total of $2,000.

Price of Stock per Share at End of Six-Month Period	Value of Call	Value of Put	Net Profit or Loss (Before Commissions)
$55	0	$10,000	+ $8,000
60	0	5,000	+ 3,000
63	0	2,000	0
65	0	0	− 2,000
70	0	0	− 2,000
75	0	0	− 2,000
77	$ 2,000	0	0
80	5,000	0	+ 3,000
85	10,000	0	+ 8,000

Note that if the stock stays at $70 a share, both your put and your call options are worthless. If the price of the stock is between $65 and $75 a share, you still lose your entire investment at the end of the six-month period.[3] As the table shows, the stock must go below $63 a share or above $77 a share for you to do anything more than break even. Beyond those numbers, of course, your profits soar. In fact, for every dollar that the stock goes above $77 a share or below $63 a share, you make $1,000 profit. If you should be so fortunate that the stock rises to $85 a share or falls to $55, you would earn $8,000, or a 400 percent return.

---

[3] Remember, you could have sold either of your options any time during the six-month period.

Bear in mind that the odds are always against you in this type of investment, for it is more than likely that this stock would have stayed at a level between $65 and $75, and your loss in this instance would be your entire investment.

There is one advantage to the option market over interest rate speculation and that is, in the option market your loss potential is limited to your original investment, whereas in the case of interest speculation, you could get stuck on a margin call and wind up having to come up with more money. If that happened and you didn't produce the extra cash, the broker would automatically sell your bonds to get the money.

Both of these types of speculations are interesting and even great fun for a good number of investors. Of course, you must know what you're doing. A good broker obviously can come in handy, but even so, it takes effort to find the best one. Since commissions vary, even finding a brokerage house takes some shopping around.

There are literally thousands of different types of speculations based on interest changes, stock movements, option markets, and the like available today. The important thing to remember before you enter into any one of these situations is that it is entirely possible for you to lose all the money you invest.

Can you live with that?

It's a question that only you can answer.

12

Toward Tomorrow

When I was a teenager, I received a few hundred dollars as part of an insurance settlement. Even at that early age, the business of investing seemed to me to hold all the riches I could imagine. I decided to put my money in the stock market. I called my father's all-knowing stockbroker and asked the same question that is asked thousands of times daily, "What's a good stock?" Without hesitation, the broker gave me the name of *the* best stock available, and of course, I bought it, at 5¾ a share. The stock would double within a short period, the broker told me. I watched and waited.

Sure enough, within two weeks the stock went up to 7⅛. "Don't sell yet," the all-knowing broker told me when I called. "It's bound to go up to 12 soon." He promised to call me when it did.

The broker never called and the stock soon went down to 3¾. "Don't sell yet," he advised me again. "You can still make back your money." Of course, I listened.

Several years later, the stock was delisted and reorganized, and I sold it—at a loss of 95 percent of my original investment and a slight tax benefit.

Money wasted? Not really, for the experience taught

me a few things about investing that I use to this day and that this book has hopefully pointed out.

The first lesson was that where investments are concerned, it is imperative that one take charge of—and accept the responsibility for—all decisions. Sure, you can spend years blaming brokers, bankers, insurance agents, and even cabdrivers for the bad advice they have given you, but those are *your* dollars you're dealing with, and no one is going to care about your financial future as much as you do. In my case, it cost me $300 to find out that my all-knowing broker did not, and that's true of anyone in the investment business.

The second lesson I learned is that investing is *always* a risk. And risk is not the problem. The problems start when you make an investment without evaluating the *level* of risk involved and your ability to withstand it. A very wise and learned man of Wall Street once wrote, "An ideal investment is totally nonexistent."[1] Furthermore, an advantageous investment for one individual may not be so for another. As we've seen in Chapter 3, people's situations vary, and it is important that any financial move be viewed from a variety of perspectives, not the least of which is a thorough evaluation of personal circumstances. It is critical, then, to know yourself and to think about whether the potential return on an investment is sufficient to compensate for the risk taken.

The third lesson I learned from my early experience was to use my mistakes to learn further, for the incident surely taught me plenty about the stock market, brokers, the value of money, and the true nature of "a sure thing." Of course, no one likes to lose, but if that is what happens to you, try to evaluate the experience and to learn from it. The knowledge you gain surely will minimize your losses.

---

[1]Gerald M. Loeb, *The Battle for Investment Survival* (New York: Simon & Schuster), 1957. Much of what Loeb said over twenty-five years ago is still relevant today.

Finally, I learned that when the chips turn downward, it is often advisable to take your loss early and get out while you still can salvage something of your initial investment. Of course, it's often difficult to admit that you've made a mistake, but bear in mind that staying in there for the long pull may very well end in a total debacle. Reevaluate your investment in light of new developments, and act accordingly.

How do you decide whether to hold on or to sell after you've made this new evaluation? Simply by asking yourself the question, Would I make that same investment today if I had the chance? If the answer is affirmative, stay with it. But if the answer is no—and the tax advantage of the loss is negligible—then get out. (Generally, tax implications should not dictate your investment decisions.) The former decision, however, should point out another aspect of investing that you must keep in mind: Notwithstanding get-rich-quick schemes, investing is generally a long-term commitment involving plenty of stamina. As a famous Englishman once wrote, "Patience is a necessary ingredient of genius." That's true, also, of wise investing, for without it, poor decisions and sad losses are imminent. Hopefully, patience will give you the staying power to see the forest through the trees.

All of these points bring me to a basic theory that can be described as *holistic investing*, which is quite analogous to the theory of holistic medicine that has been advanced greatly during the past decade and which purports that the body must be viewed as a whole; the physical and psychological aspects of humans, for instance, cannot be treated separately. My theory of holistic investing says something similar, that you cannot look at an investment simply by evaluating its effect on your wallet. What about your blood pressure and the effect of that investment—especially if it turns out to be a poor one—on your general health? As an economics professor replied when a graduate student asked him why he didn't invest in the stock market, "I like to sleep."

172

A similar story is attributed to J. P. Morgan, the famous financier. A friend of his was so worried about his investments that he could not sleep at night. Eventually this man went to Morgan for advice and asked, "What should I do about my stocks?" Morgan astutely replied, "Sell down to the sleeping point." Everyone has his or her own comfort zone. Find yours and make your investment decisions accordingly.

How *Not* to Invest $5,000

Persuasive salespeople abound, as you might already know, and as you've read through this book you may have noticed the absence of some of the advice they have offered you. It is fitting, then, that you arm yourself with information on exactly why some very common investments are not for you.

Penny stocks. These are stocks that generally can be bought for pennies a share. Thousands of shares can be purchased for a few hundred dollars. Unfortunately, however, the risks are high, and large profits are few and far between. Las Vegas or Atlantic City probably is a better bet.

Long-term bonds. As we've seen in Chapter 6, bond prices fall as interest rates rise. Since it is more than likely that interest rates will rise in the future, these are definitely not recommended. In general, staying away from investments that lock you into a given rate of return for a long period means leaving your options open, another good rule to follow.

Collectibles. By these we mean stamps, coins, antiques, fine art, and such. The market for these is highly volatile, and these investments lack any kind of decent liquidity. In this area, you must truly be an expert to authenticate purchases and know their market value. For laypeople, the risk here is entirely too great.

Precious stones. As with gold jewelry, which we have discussed briefly, you must buy these at retail prices and sell them at wholesale prices. Therefore, a substantial rise in value is necessary before you can just break even, making these investments far too risky for most investors. Again, expert knowledge is needed to ensure savvy purchases.

Strategic metals. Last year's investment fad has faded: Stay away!

Commodity futures. It's true that much money can be made here, but you need more money than the small investor has at hand to start out. Furthermore, the risk is enormous, and most people who invest in commodity futures wind up losing.

Interest-rate futures. As Chapter 11 explains, these speculations can be fun, but they're definitely not recommended for those who enjoy sleeping.

Tax-exempt municipal bonds. These are not recommended to small investors for two reasons. First, they usually are long-term investments, making the risk factor quite high. Second, their tax advantage really does not fully benefit the individual who does not have a high adjusted gross income.

Land speculation. These investments are extremely volatile and illiquid. By staying away from these, you may surely miss out on the opportunity of a lifetime, but you'll also be passing up the chance to buy swampland in Florida and a lot of other worthless properties that have been sold in the past.

Stock market. Individual stock market investments are not recommended due to a lack of diversification and the enormous risk involved. If you have faith in the stock market, you're better off putting your money in one of the no-load mutual funds described in Chapter 4. Of course, I waive my own rule about the stock market where qualified electric utility companies are concerned due to their very favorable tax advantages and stock reinvestment programs.

As you can see, the major thread running through these nonrecommendables is *risk*. Either it's too high, in some, or the potential rate of return is too low for the risk ventured. Remember these points.

As for the Future . . .

The year 1982 was one of great economic change. Interest rates for mortgages were 16 percent in January, and by the end of the year they dropped to 12 to 13 percent. Money market funds appeared at banks, the stock market reached some record highs and lows, and generally speaking, a great number of investment opportunities became available, especially for small investors. Can the events of 1982, then, help us predict future developments? Not really. All they tell us is that we're living in a rapidly changing economic environment in which, if anything, change will accelerate in the years ahead. To stay on top of things, however, you can make *flexibility* the cornerstone of your investment decisions and constantly reevaluate them in light of new developments. Remember, too, to think the unthinkable—it just may happen.

Epilogue

Whatever Happened to Henry Jones?

Like all good stories, this one has a happy ending. Henry Jones was, of course, fortunate enough to read this book, and subsequently his future brightened.

First off, he doubled the interest he was receiving on his savings by switching from his bank account to a money market fund. Then he borrowed $6,000 from his pension fund and deposited $4,000 in a bank IRA. That left $2,000.

Henry borrowed against the $8,000 cash value on the whole life insurance policy he'd had stashed away (his broker advised him against it, but these days Henry is not a man to argue with), combined it with the $2,000 he had left over from his pension fund, and made a hefty down payment on a brand-new Chevy camper in which he and Mrs. Jones drove up to Maine for an extended fishing trip. Mrs. Jones found some lovely things in the antiques shops along the way and used her new credit card to pay for them. Last I heard, they had their eye on a nice four-bedroom home. The price is a bit high, but Henry thinks he can get it down. . . .

Appendix A

How Your Income Is Taxed

In deciding whether to take part in an investment program, an understanding of how it will affect your tax picture is imperative.

Most people misunderstand the meaning of tax brackets. They assume that if you're in the 30 percent bracket, you pay 30 percent of your income in taxes. But that is incorrect; actually you pay much less than 30 percent.

Tax bracket actually refers to the percentage rate at which the *last dollar* of your income is taxed. If you are in the 30 percent tax bracket, then $0.30 of each $1.00 *in addition to your base income* (see below) is what you owe in taxes. This is quite different from 30 percent of your entire income, as we can see in Table 1. Note, there, that a married couple with a combined taxable income of $30,000 is in the 30 percent tax bracket. But they do not pay $9,000 (30 percent of $30,000) in taxes; they pay only $5,064. Their average tax rate is simply their total taxes divided by their taxable income, or, in this case:

$$\frac{\$\ 5,064}{\$30,000} = 16.9\%$$

Table 1.
Projected Tax Rate Schedule: Married Filing Joint Return

If Your Taxable Income Is Between (A)	and (B)	1983 You Pay +	% on Excess	1984 You Pay +	% on Excess
0	$ 3,400	0	0	0	0
$ 3,400	5,500	0	11	0	11
5,500	7,600	$ 231	13	$ 231	12
7,600	11,900	504	15	483	14
11,900	16,000	1,149	17	1,085	16
16,000	20,200	1,846	19	1,741	18
20,200	24,600	2,644	23	2,497	22
24,600	29,900	3,656	26	3,465	25
29,900	35,200	5,034	30	4,790	28
35,200	45,800	6,624	35	6,274	33
45,800	60,000	10,334	40	9,772	38
60,000	85,600	16,014	44	15,168	42
85,600	109,400	27,278	48	25,920	45
109,400	162,400	38,702	50	36,630	49
162,400	215,400	65,202	50	62,600	50
215,400	and up	91,702	50	89,100	50

Thus, the important fact to remember in assessing an investment, or even the possibility of taking on a second job, is whether it will place you in a higher bracket and how the higher tax due will balance against your additional income.

Let's look at a specific example:

Mr. and Mrs. George Smith have a combined total gross income of $34,500. To arrive at their total *taxable* income, they subtracted the following:

Total gross income	$34,500
Less deductions	
$5,000 (in miscellaneous deductions)	
$4,000 (for 4 dependents)	–9,000
Taxable income	$25,500

178

Table 2.
Projected Tax Rate Schedule: Single Individual Return

If Your Taxable Income Is Between (A)	and (B)	1983 You Pay +	% on Excess	1984 You Pay +	% on Excess
0	$ 2,300	0	0	0	0
$ 2,300	3,400	0	11	0	11
3,400	4,400	$ 121	13	$ 121	12
4,400	6,500	251	15	241	14
5,600	8,500	566	15	535	15
8,500	10,800	866	17	835	16
10,800	12,900	1,257	19	1,203	18
12,900	15,000	1,656	21	1,581	20
15,000	18,200	2,097	24	2,001	23
18,200	23,500	2,865	28	2,737	26
23,500	28,800	4,349	32	4,115	30
28,800	34,100	6,045	36	5,705	34
34,100	41,500	7,953	40	7,507	38
41,500	55,300	10,913	45	10,319	42
55,300	81,800	17,123	50	16,115	48
81,800	108,300	30,373	50	28,835	50
108,300	and up	43,623	50	42,085	50

Referring to Table 1, we find that for 1983 the Smiths would be required to pay $3,656 plus 26 percent of all income in excess of $24,600 (the base income), or 26 percent of $900, which amounts to $234. Thus, their total taxes would be $3,656 plus $234, which is a grand total of $3,890.

Actually, the $3,890 that the Smiths pay is only 11.3 percent of their total gross income; and the average tax rate for their taxable income of $25,500 is only 15.3 percent. The 26 percent rate referred to in Table 1 is actually a *marginal tax rate*, and it is this number that will be critical to you in making investment decisions. Thus, use Tables 1 and 2 for future financial planning.

Appendix B

The Time Value of Money, or How Money Grows

An understanding of the time value of money is an important tool in investment planning, retirement planning, or the effects of inflation or tax deferments. Basically what we're talking about here is the fact that a dollar received in the future is worth less than a dollar received today, for if you had that dollar now, you could invest it to earn additional income. The following tables should give you some ideas as to exactly how money grows over various periods and at different interest rates.

The Future Value of Money

Future value refers to the value of a sum of money invested at a specified rate after a given period of time, assuming that interest accrued along the way has been compounded, or added to the principal. Table 1 enables you to calculate the future value of an investment taking this process into account. For instance, if you place $2,000 in a bank for seven years at 12 percent interest, at the end of seven years it would be worth $2,000 x 2.21, or $4,420.

The Present Value of Money

Present value is the value of a sum received in the future if you had it now and invested it at a certain rate of interest. For instance, if you were given the choice of $5,000 today or $7,000 in five years, you would use present-value calculations in Table 2 to find that at an interest rate of 10 percent, for example, the present-value factor would be 0.6209. Multiply that by the $7,000 for a total of $4,346 and you can see that at this rate $5,000 now is worth more than $7,000 in five years.

Table 1.
Compound Interest: Value of $1.00 Compounded Annually at Rates of Return from 1 to 15% over 1 to 40 Years

Year	1%	2%	3%	4%	5%	6%	7%	8%	9%	10%	11%	12%	13%	14%	15%
1	1.01	1.02	1.03	1.04	1.05	1.06	1.07	1.08	1.09	1.10	1.11	1.12	1.13	1.14	1.15
2	1.02	1.04	1.06	1.08	1.10	1.12	1.15	1.17	1.19	1.21	1.23	1.25	1.28	1.30	1.32
3	1.03	1.05	1.09	1.13	1.16	1.19	1.23	1.26	1.30	1.33	1.37	1.41	1.44	1.48	1.52
4	1.04	1.08	1.13	1.17	1.22	1.26	1.31	1.36	1.41	1.46	1.52	1.57	1.63	1.69	1.75
5	1.05	1.10	1.16	1.22	1.28	1.34	1.40	1.47	1.54	1.61	1.69	1.76	1.84	1.93	2.01
6	1.06	1.13	1.19	1.27	1.34	1.42	1.50	1.59	1.68	1.77	1.87	1.97	2.08	2.20	2.31
7	1.07	1.15	1.23	1.32	1.41	1.50	1.61	1.71	1.83	1.95	2.08	2.21	2.35	2.50	2.66
8	1.08	1.17	1.27	1.37	1.48	1.59	1.72	1.85	1.99	2.14	2.30	2.48	2.66	2.85	3.06
9	1.09	1.20	1.31	1.42	1.55	1.69	1.84	2.00	2.17	2.36	2.56	2.77	3.00	3.25	3.52
10	1.10	1.22	1.34	1.48	1.63	1.79	1.97	2.16	2.37	2.59	2.84	3.11	3.40	3.71	4.05
11	1.12	1.24	1.38	1.54	1.71	1.90	2.11	2.33	2.58	2.85	3.15	3.48	3.84	4.23	4.65
12	1.13	1.27	1.43	1.60	1.80	2.01	2.25	2.52	2.81	3.14	3.50	3.90	4.34	4.82	5.35
13	1.14	1.29	1.47	1.67	1.89	2.13	2.41	2.72	3.07	3.45	3.88	4.36	4.90	5.49	6.15
14	1.15	1.32	1.51	1.73	1.98	2.26	2.58	2.94	3.34	3.80	4.31	4.89	5.54	6.26	7.08
15	1.16	1.35	1.56	1.80	2.08	2.40	2.76	3.17	3.64	4.18	4.79	5.47	6.25	7.14	8.14
16	1.17	1.37	1.61	1.87	2.18	2.54	2.95	3.43	3.97	4.60	5.31	6.13	7.07	8.14	9.36
17	1.18	1.40	1.65	1.95	2.29	2.69	3.16	3.70	4.33	5.05	5.90	6.87	7.99	9.28	10.76

18	1.20	1.43	1.70	2.03	2.41	2.85	3.38	4.00	4.72	5.56	6.54	7.69	9.03	10.57	12.38
19	1.21	1.46	1.75	2.11	2.53	3.03	3.62	4.32	5.14	6.12	7.26	8.61	10.20	12.06	14.23
20	1.22	1.49	1.81	2.19	2.65	3.21	3.87	4.66	5.60	6.73	8.06	9.65	11.52	13.74	16.37
21	1.23	1.52	1.86	2.28	2.79	3.40	4.14	5.03	6.11	7.40	8.94	10.80	13.02	15.67	18.82
22	1.25	1.55	1.92	2.37	2.93	3.60	4.43	5.44	6.66	8.14	9.93	12.10	14.72	17.86	21.65
23	1.26	1.58	1.97	2.46	3.07	3.82	4.74	5.87	7.26	8.96	11.03	13.55	16.63	20.36	24.89
24	1.27	1.61	2.03	2.56	3.23	4.05	5.07	6.34	7.91	9.85	12.24	15.18	18.79	23.21	28.63
25	1.28	1.64	2.09	2.67	3.39	4.29	5.43	6.85	8.62	10.84	13.59	17.00	21.23	26.46	32.92
26	1.30	1.66	2.15	2.77	3.56	4.55	5.81	7.40	9.40	11.92	15.08	19.04	23.99	30.16	37.86
27	1.31	1.69	2.22	2.88	3.73	4.82	6.21	7.99	10.25	13.11	16.74	21.33	27.11	34.39	43.54
28	1.32	1.72	2.29	3.00	3.92	5.11	6.65	8.63	11.17	14.42	18.58	23.88	30.64	39.20	50.07
29	1.33	1.76	2.36	3.12	4.12	5.42	7.12	9.06	12.17	15.86	20.62	26.75	34.62	44.69	57.58
30	1.35	1.79	2.43	3.24	4.32	5.74	7.61	9.51	13.27	17.45	22.89	29.96	39.12	50.95	66.22
31	1.36	1.83	2.50	3.37	4.54	6.09	8.15	10.27	14.46	19.20	25.41	33.56	44.20	58.08	76.15
32	1.38	1.87	2.58	3.51	4.77	6.45	8.72	11.09	15.76	21.12	28.21	37.58	49.95	66.21	87.57
33	1.39	1.90	2.65	3.65	5.00	6.84	9.33	11.98	17.18	23.23	31.31	42.09	56.44	75.48	100.71
34	1.40	1.94	2.73	3.79	5.25	7.25	9.98	12.94	18.73	25.55	34.75	47.14	63.78	86.05	115.81
35	1.42	1.98	2.81	3.95	5.52	7.69	10.68	13.98	20.41	28.11	38.58	52.80	72.07	98.09	133.18
36	1.43	2.02	2.90	4.10	5.79	8.15	11.43	15.09	22.25	30.92	43.82	59.14	81.44	111.83	153.16
37	1.45	2.06	2.99	4.27	6.08	8.64	12.23	16.30	24.25	34.01	47.53	66.23	92.03	127.48	176.13
38	1.46	2.10	3.08	4.44	6.39	9.15	13.08	17.60	26.44	37.41	52.76	74.18	103.99	145.33	202.55
39	1.47	2.14	3.17	4.62	6.71	9.70	14.00	19.01	28.82	41.15	58.56	83.08	117.51	165.67	232.94
40	1.49	2.19	3.26	4.80	7.04	10.29	14.98	20.53	31.41	45.26	65.00	93.05	132.79	188.87	267.88

Table 2.
The Present Value of Money

Period/Rate	4%	6%	8%	10%	12%	14%	16%	18%	20%	22%
1	0.9615	0.9434	0.9259	0.9091	0.8929	0.8772	0.8621	0.8475	0.8333	0.8197
2	0.9246	0.8900	0.8573	0.8264	0.7972	0.7695	0.7432	0.7182	0.6944	0.6719
3	0.8890	0.8396	0.7938	0.7513	0.7118	0.6750	0.6407	0.6086	0.5787	0.5507
4	0.8548	0.7921	0.7350	0.6830	0.6355	0.5921	0.5523	0.5158	0.4823	0.4514
5	0.8219	0.7473	0.6806	0.6209	0.5674	0.5194	0.4761	0.4371	0.4019	0.3700
6	0.7903	0.7050	0.6302	0.5645	0.5066	0.4556	0.4104	0.3704	0.3349	0.3033
7	0.7599	0.6651	0.5835	0.5132	0.4523	0.3996	0.3538	0.3139	0.2791	0.2486
8	0.7307	0.6274	0.5403	0.4665	0.4039	0.3506	0.3050	0.2660	0.2326	0.2038
9	0.7026	0.5919	0.5002	0.4241	0.3606	0.3075	0.2630	0.2255	0.1938	0.1670
10	0.6756	0.5584	0.4632	0.3855	0.3220	0.2697	0.2267	0.1911	0.1615	0.1369
11	0.6496	0.5268	0.4289	0.3505	0.2875	0.2366	0.1954	0.1619	0.1346	0.1122

12	0.6246	0.4970	0.3971	0.3186	0.2567	0.2076	0.1685	0.1372	0.1122	0.0920
13	0.6006	0.4688	0.3677	0.2897	0.2292	0.1821	0.1452	0.1163	0.0935	0.0754
14	0.5775	0.4423	0.3405	0.2633	0.2046	0.1597	0.1252	0.0985	0.0779	0.0618
15	0.5553	0.4173	0.3152	0.2394	0.1827	0.1401	0.1079	0.0835	0.0649	0.0507
16	0.5339	0.3936	0.2919	0.2176	0.1631	0.1229	0.0930	0.0708	0.0541	0.0415
17	0.5134	0.3714	0.2703	0.1978	0.1456	0.1078	0.0802	0.0600	0.0451	0.0340
18	0.4936	0.3503	0.2502	0.1799	0.1300	0.0946	0.0691	0.0508	0.0376	0.0279
19	0.4746	0.3305	0.2317	0.1635	0.1161	0.0829	0.0596	0.0431	0.0313	0.0229
20	0.4564	0.3118	0.2145	0.1486	0.1037	0.0728	0.0514	0.0365	0.0261	0.0187
21	0.4388	0.2942	0.1987	0.1351	0.0926	0.0638	0.0443	0.0309	0.0217	0.0154
22	0.4220	0.2775	0.1839	0.1228	0.0826	0.0560	0.0382	0.0262	0.0181	0.0126
23	0.4057	0.2618	0.1703	0.1117	0.0738	0.0491	0.0329	0.0222	0.0151	0.0103
24	0.3901	0.2470	0.1577	0.1015	0.0659	0.0431	0.0284	0.0188	0.0126	0.0085
25	0.3751	0.2330	0.1460	0.0923	0.0588	0.0378	0.0245	0.0160	0.0105	0.0069

Appendix C

Banks That Offer Low-Fee (or No-Fee) Credit Cards

In Chapter 2 we recommended that investors obtain low-fee (or no-fee) credit cards and that the credit these accounts afford be used appropriately—that is, that they be viewed as accessible emergency funds. The following banks offer such accounts. You will note that while most are located in the metropolitan New York City area, any U.S. resident may apply, as all transactions can be easily accomplished through the mail. You may write or call for the proper application.

Bank	Annual Fee	Type of Card*	Annual Interest Rate
First Nationwide Savings New York City, California, Florida (Fee waived with money market account or market rate checking account)	$12	V	18%
European American Bank Metropolitan New York City area (Fee waived with checking account or $250 minimum balance savings account)	$15	V/M	19.6%
Marine Midland Bank New York City (Fee reduced to $7.50 per card with Now account, Super Now account, or money market account)	$15 (for one or both cards)	V/M	19.8%
Chemical Bank Metropolitan New York City area	$15, or both for $24	V/M	19%
Goldome Bank for Savings Metropolitan New York City area and Buffalo (Fee waived with $10,000 savings deposit)	$15	V	18%
Bank of New York Metropolitan New York City area	$12	V/M	19.8%

Bank	Annual Fee	Type of Card*	Annual Interest Rate
Bank of America Western States	$12	V	19.8%
Midlantic National Bank New Jersey	$15	V/M	18%
Bankers Trust Company Metropolitan New York City area	$15	V	18%
Chase Manhattan Bank Metropolitan New York City area	$20	V	21%
Citibank Metropolitan New York City area	$20	V/M	19.8%
Irving Trust Company Metropolitan New York City area	$20	V	19.8%
Sterling National Bank Metropolitan New York City area	$15	V/M	19%

*V—Visa.
M—MasterCard.

Annuities

An annuity is a periodic payment for a specified number of periods. For instance, if you are receiving $500 a month from a pension plan, that's an annuity. Table 1 allows you to calculate how much money you would make if an annuity is invested at a given interest rate for a specified number of periods. This calculation would be useful for assessing the value of IRA investments made periodically.

Finding the future value of an annuity from Table 1 for twenty-five years at an interest rate of 12 percent, we find that $2,000 a year in contributions would amount to $266,667. According to the table, the period of twenty-five years at 12 percent shows an annuity factor of 133.3339. Multiply that by $2,000 and you arrive at the total of $266,667.

Table 1.
The Future Value of an Annuity

Period/Rate	4%	6%	8%	10%	12%	14%	16%	18%	20%	22%
1	1.0000	1.0000	1.0000	1.0000	1.0000	1.0000	1.0000	1.0000	1.0000	1.0000
2	2.0400	2.0600	2.0800	2.1000	2.1200	2.1400	2.1600	2.1800	2.2000	2.2200
3	3.1216	3.1836	3.2464	3.3100	3.3744	3.4396	3.5056	3.5724	3.6400	3.7084
4	4.2465	4.3746	4.5061	4.6410	4.7793	4.9211	5.0665	5.2154	5.3680	5.5242
5	5.4163	5.6371	5.8666	6.1051	6.3528	6.6101	6.8771	7.1542	7.4416	7.7396
6	6.6330	6.9753	7.3359	7.7156	8.1152	8.5355	8.9775	9.4420	9.9299	10.4423
7	7.8983	8.3938	8.9228	9.4872	10.890	10.7305	11.4139	12.1415	12.9159	13.7396
8	9.2142	9.8975	10.6366	11.4359	12.2997	13.2328	14.2401	15.3270	16.4991	17.7623
9	10.5828	11.4913	12.4876	13.5795	14.7757	16.0853	17.5185	19.0859	20.7989	22.6700
10	12.0061	13.1808	14.4866	15.9374	17.5487	19.3373	21.3215	23.5213	25.9587	28.6574
11	13.4864	14.9716	16.6455	18.5312	20.6546	23.0445	25.7329	28.7551	32.1504	35.9620

12	15.0258	16.8699	18.9771	21.3843	24.1331	27.2707	30.8502	34.9311	39.5805	44.8737
13	16.6268	18.8821	21.4953	24.5227	28.0291	32.0887	36.7862	42.2187	48.4966	55.7459
14	18.2919	21.0151	24.2149	27.9750	32.3926	37.5811	43.6720	50.8180	59.1959	69.0100
15	20.0236	23.2760	27.1521	31.7725	37.2797	43.8424	51.6595	60.9653	72.0351	85.1922
16	21.8245	25.6725	30.3243	35.9497	42.7533	50.9804	60.9250	72.9390	87.4421	104.9345
17	23.6975	28.2129	33.7502	40.5447	48.8837	59.1176	71.6730	87.0680	105.9306	129.0201
18	25.6454	30.9057	37.4502	45.5992	55.7497	68.3941	84.1407	103.7403	128.1167	158.4045
19	27.6712	33.7600	41.4463	51.1591	63.4397	78.9692	98.6032	123.4135	154.7400	194.2535
20	29.7781	36.7856	45.7620	57.2750	72.0524	91.0249	115.3797	146.6280	186.6880	237.9893
21	31.9692	39.9927	50.4229	64.0025	81.6987	104.7684	134.8405	174.0210	225.0256	291.3469
22	34.2480	43.3923	55.4568	71.4028	92.5026	120.4360	157.4150	206.3448	271.0307	356.4432
23	36.6179	46.9958	60.8933	79.5430	104.6029	138.2970	183.6014	244.4868	326.2369	435.8603
24	39.0826	50.8156	66.7648	88.4973	118.1552	158.6586	213.9776	289.4945	392.4842	532.7501
25	41.6459	54.8645	73.1059	98.3471	133.3339	181.8708	249.2140	342.6035	471.9811	650.9551

Glossary

adjustable-rate mortgage (ARM) A mortgage whose interest rate changes according to interest-rate market conditions.

aggressive growth fund A mutual fund whose main goal is the maximum growth of assets with commensurate risk and little attention to current income. Also known as *maximum capital gains fund* and *performance fund*.

assets Any property that has value and is owned. It may be tangible (such as a building) or intangible (such as a patent).

bear market A market in which the price trend is declining.

bull market A market in which the price trend is rising.

buy-down The purchase, usually by a seller, of a reduction in the bank mortgage interest rate for a specified time and amount of money.

call The right to buy shares of a particular stock, if desired, at a set price for a given period.

capital gains The profit received by selling an asset that has been held for more than one year. This profit is taxed more favorably (lower) as a capital gain.

certificate of deposit A short-term obligation of a commercial bank, usually negotiable at a specified interest rate and for a specified period.

commercial paper A short-term, negotiable obligation of a major corporation at a specified interest rate and for a specified time.

credit union A financial organization whose members are drawn from some specific group (such as employees of a company, teachers, or firemen) and created to receive savings from the members to be loaned to other members at reasonable rates of interest.

current yield The rate of return, expressed in percentage, obtained by dividing an annual dollar return by the current market price of a bond. For example:

$$\frac{\$100}{\$1,000} = 10\%$$

dividend growth rate The average annual rate of increase of dividends over a specified period.

effective annual yield The annual rate of return based upon simple interest compounded annually.

growing-equity mortgage (GEM) A mortgage in which the amount of the principal paid increases at a set rate each year.

growth stock mutual fund A mutual fund whose goal is to invest in companies that are generally growing faster than the economy.

Keogh plan A plan for self-employed people to invest a percentage of their income for retirement after age 59½. The savings and earnings are tax-deferred during the accumulation period.

leverage Using a small amount of funds to control a much larger asset. Leverage helps accentuate both profits and losses.

liability Debt owed to a creditor.

liquidity The ease with which an asset can be converted into cash with the least possibility of loss of a portion of the funds.

load A commission.

load fund A mutual fund that charges a sales commission.

margin Purchase of securities partly with borrowed money, usually obtained from a broker.

maximum capital gains mutual fund See *aggressive growth fund*. These terms are interchangeable.

money market mutual fund A mutual fund that generally invests only in treasury bills, commercial paper, and certificates of deposit.

mutual fund A company that sells shares to investors and uses the money to pursue certain investment goals. Formally known as an *investment company*.

net asset value (NAV) The number obtained by adding all net assets and dividing the total by the number of shares outstanding. This is the price obtained in selling or having mutual fund shares.

no-load fund A mutual fund that charges no sales commission.

option The right to buy or sell an asset (for example, a stock) at a specified price for a specified period. See *put*; also see *call*.

par value Referring to bonds, the value of a bond at maturity.

performance fund See *aggressive growth fund*. These terms are interchangeable.

principal A sum of money that is borrowed and then owed, as opposed to interest.

purchase money mortgage A mortgage issued by a seller to a buyer of real estate.

put An option to sell an asset (for example, a stock) for a specified price for a specified period.

second mortgage A junior lien or claim to a first mortgage against real estate. A second mortgage generally has a higher interest rate and is of shorter duration than the first mortgage.

seller financing A situation in which the seller of real estate agrees to give the buyer a first and/or second mortgage to enable the buyer to make the purchase.

special situation fund A mutual fund whose investment goal is to seek out special circumstances that will favorably affect a stock (for example, company reorganization).

straddle   The simultaneous purchase of a put and a call on the same stock.

treasury bill   A short-term obligation of the U.S. government issued in three-, six-, and twelve-month maturities.

treasury bond   A long-term obligation of the U.S. government issued in maturities that usually range from ten to thirty years.

treasury note   An intermediate obligation of the U.S. government issued in maturities that range from two to seven years.

Index

198

ABOUT THE AUTHORS

EDWARD MALCA received his B.B.A. from the City College of New York, his M.B.A. from Baruch College, and his Ph.D. in Economics and Finance from the City University of New York. From 1970 until 1973, he taught graduate faculty courses at Baruch College in Advanced Investment Analysis, Money and Banking, and Corporate Finance and Business Policy. From 1973 until 1980 he was Assistant Professor of Economics and Finance at The College of Staten Island (CUNY), where he also acted as coordinator of business programs.

For the past ten years, Dr. Malca has been offering a series of highly successful seminars to Con Edison employees on Financial Planning for the Small Investor and on Preretirement Planning. These lectures and workshops have achieved an overwhelming level of popularity within the company.

In 1974, Dr. Malca testified as an expert witness on the subject of pension and bank trust department investment policies before the U.S. Senate Finance Committee.

Dr. Malca's published books include: *Pension and Institutional Portfolio Management* (Praeger, 1976); *Pension Funds and Other Institutional Investors* (Lexington Books, 1975); and *Bank Administered Commingled Pension Funds* (Lexington Books, 1973).

As President of the Malca Investment Advisory Service, Dr. Malca has lectured widely and currently consults with a number of private clients. He lives in Teaneck, New Jersey.

SANDRA CHORON graduated from Lehman College in 1971 and then worked for over ten years as an editor in book publishing, first for Hawthorn Books and then for Dell Publishing. She currently heads her own book producing firm and is a literary agent as well as a writer. Ms. Choron is associate editor of a newsletter titled *Dave Marsh's Rock & Roll Confidential* and a member of the board of directors of the American Book Producers Association. She lives in Teaneck, New Jersey.

MONEY TALKS!
How to get it and How to keep it!

☐	23991	NO BULL SELLING by Hank Trisler	$3.50
☐	23716	I.B.M. COLOSSUS IN TRANSITION by Robert Sobel	$4.95
☐	23586	BERNARD MELTZER SOLVES YOUR MONEY PROBLEMS by Bernard Meltzer	$3.95
☐	23489	SALARY STRATEGIES by Marilyn Moats Kennedy	$3.50
☐	23913	ALL YOU NEED TO KNOW ABOUT BANKS by John Cook & Robert Wool	$3.95
☐	23568	GET A JOB IN 60 SECONDS by Steve Kravette	$2.95
☐	22509	THE BOOK OF FIVE RINGS by Miyamoto Musashi	$2.95
☐	22936	HOW TO GET FREE TAX HELP by Matthew Lesko	$2.95
☐	23455	YOU CAN NEGOTIATE ANYTHING by Herb Cohen	$3.95
☐	24138	GUERRILLA TACTICS IN THE JOB MARKET by T. Jackson	$3.95
☐	23563	THE ONLY INVESTMENT GUIDE YOU'LL EVER NEED by Andrew Tobias	$3.95
☐	24558	HOW TO WAKE UP THE FINANCIAL GENIUS INSIDE YOU by Mark Oliver Haroldsen	$3.95
☐	23099	THE GAMESMAN: The New Corporate Leaders by Michael Maccoby	$3.95
☐	22909	THE GREATEST SALESMAN IN THE WORLD by Og Mandino	$2.75
☐	22550	ALMOST EVERYONE'S GUIDE TO ECONOMICS by Galbraith/Salinge	$2.95
☐	20191	HIGH FINANCE ON A LOW BUDGET by Mark Skousen	$2.95

Prices and availability subject to change without notice.

Buy them at your local bookstore or use this handy coupon for ordering:

Bantam Books, Inc., Dept. MSP, 414 East Golf Road, Des Plaines, Ill 60016

Please send me the books I have checked above. I am enclosing $_____
(please add $1.25 to cover postage and handling). Send check or money order
—no cash or C.O.D.'s please.

Mr/Mrs/Miss_____

Address_____

City_____ State/Zip_____

MSP—6/84

Please allow four to six weeks for delivery. This offer expires 12/84.

BANTAM IS PLUGGED IN TO COMPUTERS

☐ 34086	Bowker/Bantam 1984 Complete Sourcebook of Personal Computing (A Large Format Book)	$18.95
☐ 23705	Easyguide For The TI99 4A— Cloverdale Press	$3.95
☐ 23706	Easyguide For The IBM PC— Cloverdale Press	$3.95
☐ 23707	Easyguide For The Apple 11E— Cloverdale Press	$3.95
☐ 23873	The Complete Buyer's Guide to Personal Computers—Tim Hartnell	$4.95
☐ 23871	The Illustrated Computer Dictionary— Editors of Consumer Guide	$3.95
☐ 23242	Mastering Your Timex Sinclair 1000 Personal Computer—Tim Hartnell & Dilwyn Jones	$3.95
☐ 22863	Electronic Cottage—Joseph Deken	$3.95
☐ 23872	The Simple Guide to Understanding Computers—Eugene Brown	$3.95

Prices and availability subject to change without notice.

Buy them at your local bookstore or use this handy coupon for ordering:

Bantam Books, Inc., Dept. CM, 414 East Golf Road, Des Plaines, Ill. 60016

Please send me the books I have checked above. I am enclosing $_____ (please add $1.25 to cover postage and handling). Send check or money order—no cash or C.O.D.'s please.

Mr/Ms_____

Address_____

City State_____ Zip_____

CM—6/84

Please allow four to six weeks for delivery. This offer expires 12/84.

SPECIAL
MONEY SAVING
OFFER

Now you can have an up-to-date listing of
Bantam's hundreds of titles plus take advantage
of our unique and exciting bonus book offer. A
special offer which gives you the opportunity to
purchase a Bantam book for only 50¢. Here's
how!

By ordering any five books at the regular price
per order, you can also choose any other single
book listed (up to a $4.95 value) for just 50¢.
Some restrictions do apply, but for further de-
tails why not send for Bantam's listing of titles
today!

Just send us your name and address plus 50¢
to defray the postage and handling costs.

BANTAM BOOKS, INC.
Dept. FC, 414 East Golf Road, Des Plaines, Ill 60016

Mr./Mrs./Miss/Ms. _____
(please print)

Address _____

City_____ State_____ Zip_____
FC—3/84